CONTENTS

MOVING PEOPLE, TRANSPORTING GOODS

NEW TECHNIQUES OF REPRESENTATION

LOOKING FORWARD

REFLECTIONS FOR THE FUTURE

FOREWORD

Sean Chiao, AECOM

How can we fundamentally rethink urban development to integrate the yet largely unexplored potential space? Can we build more livable, authentic, better connected and resilient cities?

There are multiple reference points for what has traditionally been defined as "underground." But where exactly is the ground? The limits of what lies above and below have never been less clear. In our cities, the underground could begin at -5m or, equally, at +6m. In the past, 3m was considered deep. Now technology allows us to excavate much further, so buildings can be occupied many stories below ground.

Over time natural and man-made systems causing great destruction have pushed us not only to rebuild but also to rethink our methods. With advances in technology and the invention of new materials and tools, what is feasible enters a different dimension. It is time to redefine the underground.

Throughout the twentieth century soaring skyscrapers such as Frank Lloyd Wright's "Mile High Illinois" or the 125-story "Miglin-Beitler Skyneedle" were conceptualized and designed, but the public appetite for living and working at those heights had not yet caught up. Today, the opposite is true. Designs such as the

35-story cylindrical "Depthscraper," meant to withstand Japan's large-scale earthquakes, or the "Earthscraper," intended for the crowded historic center of Mexico City, may be in a similar place of waiting. The design concept, feasibility and technology are there. What is lacking is a sense of immediacy.

In the twenty-first century, climate change, rapid urbanization and resource depletion are forcing everyone to reconsider what is essential about our living spaces. It is imperative to adapt to this new reality and creatively explore the full potential of sustainably maximizing our land use.

What does this mean for the future of collective living?

We must seek to build strong, resilient communities with people at their core. My hope is that by casting light beyond our current perception of uses for space, Underground Cities will energize and inspire a transformation within our industry. There are tremendous opportunities on the horizon for those who think creatively about the underground. May the pages that follow spark a sense of wonder and curiosity about the depths below and ignite a drive to explore all the untapped potential it holds.

A NEW FRONTIER

The last 50 years have seen a radical shift in the conception of the underground. No longer just a place to hide infrastructure, it is increasingly being explored as a means of supporting sustainable urban development — a reservoir of much-needed land and of resources such as geothermal energy. "A New Frontier" traces the emergence of this underground urbanism through the example of two pioneering cities, Montreal and Helsinki, and two visionary 1960s schemes inspired by a growing environmental consciousness, Minnesota Experimental City and Guy Rottier's Ecopolis. Suggesting new possibilities for the "deep city," it invites reflection on how the pace of technological change is bringing within our reach ideas that not so long ago seemed utopian. As importantly, it shows how we need idealists as much as realists.

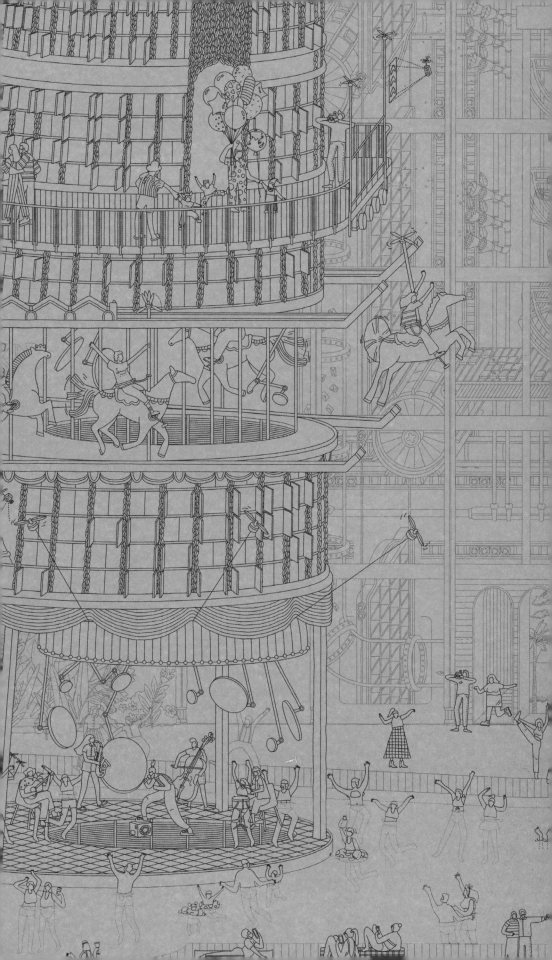

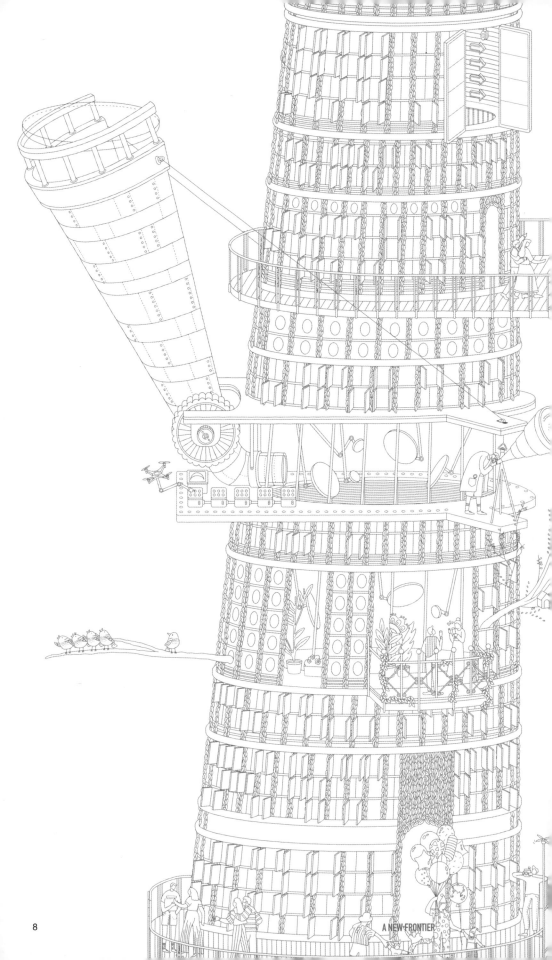

A NEW·FRONTIER

EXPERIMENTAL CITIES

Pamela Johnston

The idea of the underground as an inhabited layer of the city began to take root in the 1960s and 1970s as an extension of new metro rail systems designed to ease congestion and pollution at street level. But those same decades also saw the emergence of contemporary environmentalism and, with it, an extraordinary upwelling of visionary schemes in which the underground was not merely a conduit for transit but the indispensable base for a wholesale reimagining of the form of the city. This text samples two projects from those heady years, which seek in different ways to create high-density urban forms that are in tune with nature, recognizing that "everything is recycled and everything is limited." With the revival of interest in blank-slate planning, whether for eco-cities, smart cities or cloud towns, these projects have a resonance today, especially as the environmental and urban issues they address, far from abating, have become even more acute.

> " We have reached a point in human history where we are preparing to descend below the surface of the Earth forever … We have always lived below the surface, beneath the atmospheric ocean, in a closed, sealed, finite environment, where everything is recycled and everything is limited. Until now, we have not felt like underground dwellers because the natural system of the globe has seemed so large in comparison with any systems we might construct. That is changing. What is commonly called environmental consciousness could be described as subterranean consciousness — the awareness that we are in a very real sense not on the Earth but inside it. "

Rosalind Williams
Notes from the Underground (MIT Press, 1990)

MXC: Minnesota Experimental City

In the early 1960s American cities seemed locked in a spiral of decline, dragged down by pollution, decaying infrastructure and the violence of segregation. But Athelstan Spilhaus (1911–1998) had a solution: a prototype for a city built around the principle of total recycling, with the ultimate aim of eliminating pollution and restoring the balance between people and nature. For Spilhaus, waste was just a resource "we haven't learned yet to use." He envisioned his city as a work in progress, constantly remaking itself based on feedback from an "information utility … possibly with point-to-point video and other broadband communication."[1] As technological or social change made a building obsolete, its re-usable modular components would be absorbed into the city's sub-structure, melting away "like uneaten ice cream in a cone." Industrial symbiosis would ensure a closed loop exchange of energy and materials. Water of different qualities

below: Athelstan Spilhaus used his widely syndicated "Our New Age" Sunday comic strip to air his ideas for the Minnesota Experimental City in 1966. Image courtesy of Athelstan Spilhaus Papers, Dolph Briscoe Center for American History, University of Texas at Austin

would be used multiple times: "we never use up any water; it just carries nutrients and flushes heat and waste from our systems." No polluting internal combustion engines would be allowed within the city limits; instead, a mass transit system with "pneumatically or electrically driven small pods" would run noiselessly along elevated tracks to computer-controlled destinations, while first-mile/last-mile connections to national transport networks would be provided by dual-mode guideways that carried individual cars and service vehicles through underground corridors with fume sewers. And "just as garages can be housed under parks," Spilhaus wrote, "all services can be underground, even to the extent of going hundreds of feet down for heavy manufacturing, storage of storm water and snow and waste heat." Subterranean "utilidors" — accessible combined service and traffic tunnels — would "abat[e] the noisy digging up and remaking of streets."

There are some parallels between Spilhaus's vision of the Minnesota Experimental City (MXC) and an earlier utopian tradition inspired by Saint-Simon and Fourier. Like Fourier's prototypical phalanstery, the MXC was removed from the outside world — Spilhaus wanted a 100-mile insulating belt to prevent "conventional uncontrolled encroachments" from "nullify[ing] the experiment." An exchange of ideas, rather than material goods, would propel his city of the future. There would be no private ownership, no unbridled consumerism: "In recycling, the consumer becomes a user, which he has, in fact, always been. He essentially 'rents' everything." Ultimately, the MXC would be not only a testing ground for new technologies but also, in the spirit of Fourier and Saint-Simon, "a magnificent laboratory for ongoing social experiments" carried out under the benevolent eye of a scientific and industrial elite.

What set the MXC apart from the Fourierist self-contained community was its scale. To preserve the advantages of high-density living

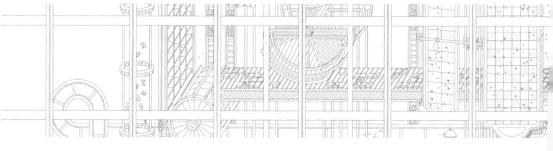

Spilhaus proposed a city of 250,000 people. Rather vaguely, he thought this might represent a cross-section of the US population, with individuals selected mainly for their willingness to tolerate "constant rearrangement without any emotional attachments to the past." Spilhaus was also somewhat hazy about the practicalities of realizing his vision. It was not clear, for example, how the city might feed itself. He thought there could perhaps be a combination of "hobby farms" and intensive farming in the surrounding area, and that dairy cows "could be fed in high-rise sterile buildings at the edge of the city to ensure the freshest, purest milk." But he might be forgiven this lack of command of detail, as this was his first foray into urban planning. His main sphere of activity was science. An aeronautical engineer, geophysicist, oceanographer and inventor of the bathythermograph (an indispensable aid to submarine warfare), he was also Dean of the Institute of Technology at Minnesota University, a member of the technical panel for NASA's Earth satellite program and the author, from 1957 on, of a widely syndicated newspaper comic strip, "Our New Age," in which most of the MXC innovations made their first public appearance.

Perhaps the most astonishing thing about this visionary city was the fact that, for a few years, it looked like it might actually be built. Championed by Otto Silha, publisher of the Minneapolis Star and Tribune, the MXC was promoted in a nationally syndicated five-part newspaper series. With the support of then Vice President Hubert Humphrey, a former Senator for Minnesota, the project secured US$250,000 in federal funding, and to guide it to the next stage Spilhaus and Silha assembled a heavyweight national steering committee that included a retired four-star general, a prominent civil rights leader, the president's personal physician, and the architect R. Buckminster Fuller, who proposed to enclose the entire city in a giant glass geodesic dome (reprising an earlier scheme for Manhattan). Spilhaus appreciated the cachet Fuller brought to the

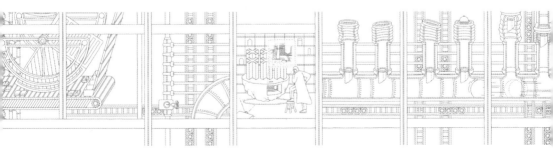

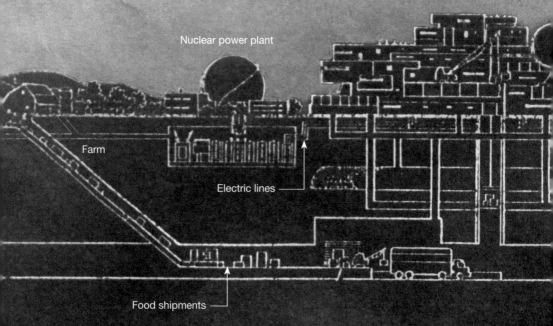

Nuclear power plant

Farm

Electric lines

Food shipments

UTILIDORS
Utility Corridor System

Proposed underground
structure of the MXC.
Courtesy of Chad Freidrichs
(dir.), "The Experimental City"
documentary, 2017

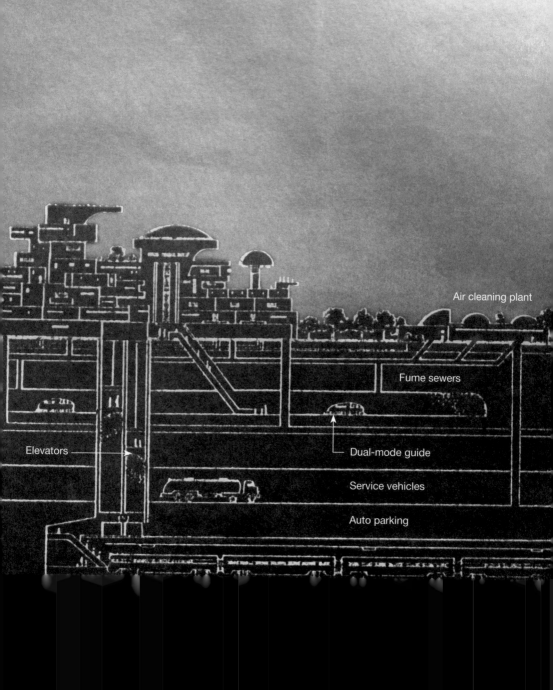

Air cleaning plant

Fume sewers

Dual-mode guide

Elevators

Service vehicles

Auto parking

project. He seemed less happy about lengthy committee meetings, with their real-world agendas and decision-making, murmuring: "When asked to talk for one hour, Fuller talked for three." In 1968, his enthusiasm for the project eroded, he resigned as co-chair of the MXC committee. There was a further setback later that year when Hubert Humphrey lost his presidential bid. The new Republican administration, under Richard Nixon, proved to be far less sympathetic to the scheme.

Still, the MXC soldiered on. The projected completion date was now 1984 and the price tag some US$10 billion. Major corporations, including Honeywell, Ford and Boeing, pledged support. A 55,000-acre site was found in swampy Central Minnesota. While this was not an ideal setting, it had the perceived advantage of being sparsely populated. But the MXC committee had not counted on the strength of opposition from local people, who immediately began a campaign of resistance, supported by environmental activists. When protestors marched 200 miles to the State Capitol in December 1972, braving temperatures of –34C, the fate of the project was sealed.

Although MXC was officially defunded and wound up in April 1973, Spilhaus never entirely let go of his dream. Later in life, he proposed a new tabula rasa site for his city — under the sea, where the "anti-engineering" lobby, with their "nonsense emotionalism," could not touch it.

66 We think the future is more beautiful than the past. Architecture is to be invented just as a car or a plane is invented … It has to be free. 99

Guy Rottier
Engineer and architect

Ecopolis, 1970
Guy Rottier (1922–2013) trained as both an engineer and an architect. After a highly auspicious start to his career, working with such luminaries as Le Corbusier, Vladimir Bodiansky and Jean Prouvé, he increasingly turned his back on commercial practice, preferring instead the freedom to explore ideas — which might be "good or bad, beautiful or ugly, saleable or not," but had to be "generally realizable." The only architect among the artists who made up the School of Nice, he was also from the mid-1960s a member of GIAP, the international group for prospective architecture. "We think the future is more

beautiful than the past," Rottier said. "Architecture is to be invented just as a car or a plane is invented … It has to be free."[2]

Rottier's first forays into the underground were on a small scale, in the form of a series of buried houses (*maisons enterrées*) he developed between 1965 and 1978. This was earth-sheltered housing adapted to the techniques of industrial production and the detritus of a consumerist society. It was not laboriously excavated out of the ground, but rather formed around a framework of prefabricated concrete or steel tubes, tiled like dominoes to give a variety of individual layouts, and then covered with earth using a bulldozer. The advantage of this, Rottier explained, was that "the architecture is no longer visible, the facades are transformed into a garden … nature engulfs all parts of the house." Also, "the materials used to cover the house are not limited to plants and earth. They can be infinitely varied, and there's nothing to stop you using recycled materials (rubble, railway sleepers, old cars, and so on). When combined in an artistic manner, these materials would "give your home an unusual or exceptional aspect that expresses your personality."[3]

For the buried house that he had Rottier build for him in Vence, France, the painter and sculptor Arman expressed his personality by choosing a decorative cladding of metal drums from scrapped washing machines. Here, a reinforced concrete slab forms a bridge between two hills, sheltering 100m^2 of living space open to the north and south. Set deeper into the slope is a windowless bedroom — the sculptor had a difficult relationship with sleep. The room is absolutely dark at night, but lit naturally for three hours a day by a "lumiduc," a light duct with reflective inner walls linked to a mirror-sensor. Applied on a larger scale — so that it could transport sunlight to any part of a large building, and even into the depths of the Earth — this device sparked the idea of Ecopolis, the solar city that Rottier developed in collaboration with the heliophysicist Maurice Touchais.

While the project was undoubtedly given impetus by Rottier's move to Damascus in 1970 to take up a long-term teaching post, his interest in solar architecture can be dated back to the late 1940s, and specifically to the three years he spent working for Le Corbusier on the Marseille Unité d'Habitation.[4] That pioneering apartment block, and all the Unités that followed, had its long axis running north–south, with east-facing bedrooms and west-facing living rooms — the scientific optimum orientation, according to the heliotherapeutic principles embedded into the larger agenda of modern architecture with the Athens Charter of 1933/41.

There are echoes of Le Corbusier's exhortations — "To introduce the sun is the new and most imperative duty of the architect" and

Guy Rottier, *Maison enterrée, "automobile carcasses,"* 1972. Paint and ink on paper, 50 x 50cm. Rottier's first foray into underground construction was a series of "buried houses" made with recycled materials — in this instance junkyard automobiles. Collection Frac Centre-Val de Loire, Guy Rottier Archive

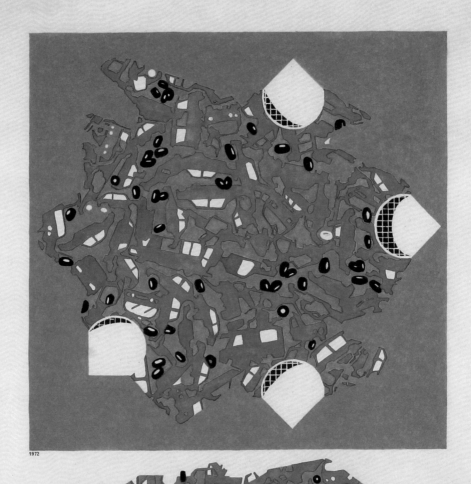

"the sun is the master of life" — in Rottier's description of his solar research, which sought to use the properties of sunlight as a "source of light and life" rather than convert it into other forms of energy. However, Rottier believed that the use of lumiducs rendered ideas about orientation outdated.

"Traditional urban planning and architecture are pollutants, because they inhibit the proper distribution of sunlight," Rottier wrote. "Our agglomerations have undifferentiated functions, and their quantity of sunlight is insufficient for their respective needs. Indeed, in today's cities, 25 percent of volumes need sunlight (e.g. dwellings, schools, hospitals), 25 percent of volumes require intermittent sunlight (offices, patios), 50 percent of volumes do not require sunlight (cinemas, supermarkets, garages). Better distribution of sunlight across these volumes is a priority."[5] His Ecopolis, conceived for a population of 25,000 (one-tenth the size of Spilhaus's MXC), was not a city of streets, squares and blocks but rather an "inhabitable green hill" with a continuous system of collective spaces organized in accordance with their requirement for light. While the important detail of how you might actually move from one space to another was not specified, this was a "generally realizable idea" for a compact vertical city.

The End of Utopia

It could be said that 1973 marked the end of an era, and not just for the Minnesota Experimental City, which was defunded, or for Rottier's Ecopolis, which had its last public outing at a UNESCO international congress on "Sun in the Service of Mankind," convened in response to the OPEC oil crisis. Writing that same year, Italian architectural critic Manfredo Tafuri declared that urban utopianism was dead. In society at large, decades of post-war experimentation had provoked increasing skepticism toward blank-slate planning, and the idea of building a city from scratch as a place to prototype the future — even to lay down the foundations of a new civilization — had come to seem less like a desirable ambition and more like megalomania. Architecture, Tafuri lamented, had lost any "revolutionary" aim and reverted to "pure architecture, to form without Utopia; in the best cases, to sublime uselessness."[6]

But perhaps the time for the "revolutionary" city has come again — if not as a comprehensive model for the way we will live in the future, then at least as an initial platform for debate. How, for example, should coastal cities adapt to rising sea levels? Athelstan Spilhaus clearly signaled the catastrophic consequences of global warming in a widely syndicated comic strip from 1958: "WE LIVE IN A GREENHOUSE! … We keep adding carbon dioxide to the air … The Earth's surface may someday warm up enough to melt the polar ice — which would raise the sea level and submerge coastal cities and low-lying plains." In the intervening 60 years, human actions have accelerated, rather than mitigated, this process. Spilhaus also railed against the excesses of a throwaway society: "each of us 'wastes' an average of 200 pounds of wrapping paper and hundreds of pounds of scrap metal per year." He did not foresee the inexorable rise of plastic packaging, which is extremely cheap to manufacture and very hard to unmake. Nor did food feature on Spilhaus's list of evils, although it now saturates many cities' waste streams.

It is the capacity to accommodate rapid change that differentiates Spilhaus's MXC — on paper at least — from some of the present generation of meticulously planned demonstration cities. "New materials would give architects a tremendous scope for developing new forms," Spilhaus wrote. The architect's main task, however, was not to create a showcase for design but to "provide new ways for people to find face-to-face relationships in an environment that does not require wasteful movement." Vitally, Spilhaus's vision of the city allowed for chance encounters — for activities that fell between the cracks of the master plan. Describing the survey mechanisms that would inform the city's flexible adaptation, he observed that in the wrong hands they "would provide a potent coercive weapon against any individual. We cannot not use such devices, although we must set up adequate safeguards against their misuse." This is an issue we still haven't resolved, as we enter the early implementation phase of a predictive tech revolution that is spawning new cloud towns and smart cities.

It seems that even unrealized utopias have something to tell us. "We have to invent the future, not just submit to it," Guy Rottier said. The truth is, we're already determining our future today. We need to keep on thinking ahead, inventing better ways of living. Taking our cue from Spilhaus, how would we imagine re-engineering the contemporary city to make it completely self-sufficient in its vital needs, recycling everything it produces, going so far as to build new structures out of waste and carving more space out of the underground?

Guy Rottier, Ecopolis, 1970.
Collage and colored pencil
on paper, 50 x 65cm. Section
through the solar city showing
lumiducs bringing light deep
below the natural terrain.
Collection Frac Centre-Val de
Loire, Guy Rottier Archive

espaces

habitables

lumiducs

paysage naturel

MONTREAL: THE VILLE INTERIEURE AS PROTOTYPE FOR THE CONTINUOUS INTERIOR

Mark Pimlott, Delft University of Technology

Promenade des boutiques,
Place Ville-Marie, Montreal,
1962. Architects I.M. Pei &
Associates. Photo George
Cserna photographs and papers,
1937–1978, Avery Architectural
& Fine Arts Library © Columbia
University in the City of New York

In Montreal there is a rambling network of passageways that now extends over 35km, most of it underground. Connecting shops, restaurants, malls, subway stations, office buildings, theaters, concert halls, art galleries and museums, conference centers and even public squares, this far from homogeneous set of passages has a long-established identity as an interior city or "ville intérieure." A refuge from cold northern winters, its qualities are deeply familiar to Montreal's citizens. Despite the banality of much of the network, it is a kind of home for its users — as natural, even in its evident artificiality, as the city's streets above ground. Distributed among the less special spaces, there are episodes associated with infrastructural nodes, public buildings and more openly public interiors that could be called both distinct and even beautiful, compelling both in their appearances and their atmospheres of freedom.

above: Promenade des boutiques, Place Ville-Marie,
Montreal, 1962. Photo Joseph W. Molitor architectural
photographs, 1935–1985, Avery Architectural & Fine Arts
Library © Columbia University in the City of New York

right: Plan showing pedestrian level of Montreal's multi-
level downtown core, 1967. Urban planner Vincent Ponte,
architects I.M. Pei & Partners. Pei Cobb Freed & Partners

Constructed from the 1960s on, this interior city appeared at a brief
period of immense change in the city, its form, its infrastructure, its
image of itself and its sense of its place in the world. What grew was
the prototype for a new kind of urban space equivalent, in its own
way, to the development of the networks of arcades or passages in
early nineteenth-century Paris. Moving through this continuous public
interior suggested the experience of walking across a landscape,
uninterrupted by crossings.

Ville Intérieure — Interior City
The network's origins are in a project for a multi-level downtown
core, built around the city's Central Station as a corrective
measure and a development opportunity. In 1955 the chairman of
the Canadian National Railway, Donald Gordon, commissioned
the New York-based property developer William Zeckendorf to
generate a master plan for a site, a deep railway cutting, that had
been long seen as a hole in the city's fabric. Under Zeckendorf's
direction, the architects I.M. Pei & Associates — who had formerly
worked in-house for his company Webb & Knapp — made a plan
for the three city blocks running north–south. These traversed
a perpendicular escarpment separating the lower historical city
center, containing the main financial district and the port on the
St. Lawrence River, from the upper part of the town, which was
the commercial center and nascent central business district. The
Ville-Marie site formed a potential bridge between the lower and

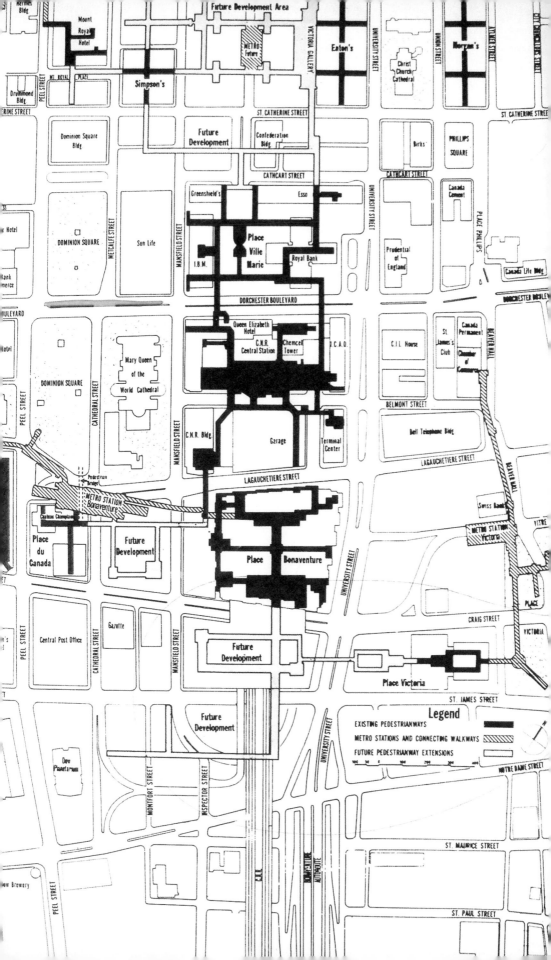

below: Perspectival section of
Place Bonaventure. Architects
ARCOP/Affleck Desbarats
Dimakopoulos Lebensold
Sise. Writing in the mid-1970s,
Reyner Banham described
Montreal as the first "mega-
city" and Place Bonaventure
as a true megastructure. Image
from Horizon, Winter 1970

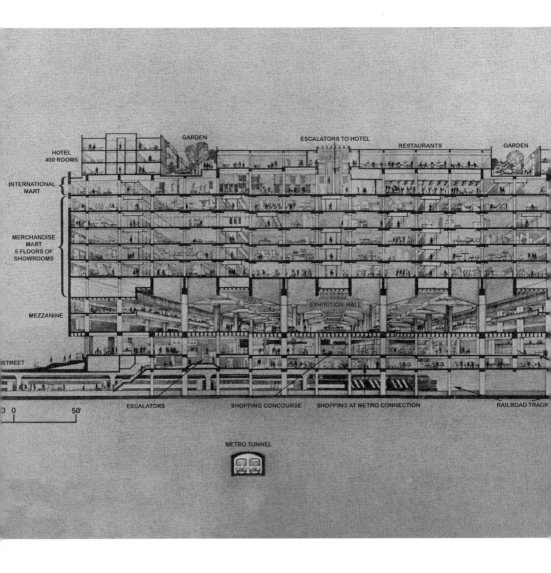

A NEW FRONTIER

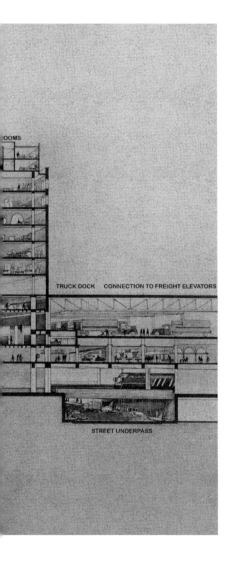

OOMS

TRUCK DOCK   CONNECTION TO FREIGHT ELEVATORS

STREET UNDERPASS

upper centers, and its architects saw the opportunity for it to be a new, elaborate and representative heart of the city. Pei and his main collaborators on this project — his young partner Henry N. Cobb and the urban planner Vincent Ponte — seemed to be ideally placed in this task. They had all come out of Harvard and were connected to the discourse on urban design developing there around Josep Lluís Sert.[1]

Multi-level Core as Idea and Image

The project that emerged from their master plan was a very dense construction both above and below ground. Its central idea was that a downtown core should work on the principle of "congestion"[2] in three dimensions, incorporating all significant infrastructure, existing and new. Its aim was to resolve the complexities of infrastructural conditions around the site at local and regional levels and provide maximum potential for commercial occupancy, with access and pedestrian movement through a large-scale structure whose most complex aspects would be underground. The project was to be a means towards the growth of the city's downtown, providing foundations for further orders or systems of related or connected infrastructure, developments and uses.

above: Place Ville-Marie,
Montreal. Architects I.M. Pei &
Associates. Photo Joseph W.
Molitor, architectural photographs,
1935–1985, Avery Architectural
& Fine Arts Library © Columbia
University in the City of New York

The underground part of this structure concentrated on the distribution of transport, goods and people across and through the site and the articulation of distinct circulation routes. An ideal city proposed by Leonardo da Vinci that separated servicing and pedestrian movement in layers (c.1480) was an important point of reference,[3] as were visionary schemes in which urban traffic played a central role, such as Eugène Hénard's sections and plans for metropolitan Paris (1890–1910),[4] Antonio Sant'Elia's Città Nuova (1914) and Harvey Wiley Corbett's hypothetical proposals for a multi-level Manhattan (1927).[5] New York City's Grand Central Terminal (Whitney Warren and Charles Wetmore, 1913) was held in high regard for its division of layers of tracks for suburban, regional and continental trains, its distribution of complex programs and integration with the street system, and its management of people to and from many directions through its representative public interior.[6] Similarly, the architects admired Rockefeller Center, New York (Raymond Hood et al., 1932), an enclave of varied function tied together by the design of buildings and public spaces both above ground and below street level.

A Three-Dimensional Urban Plan
The Ville-Marie Master Plan of 1955[7] effectively reappraised the performance of the two-part city center and demonstrated a deep understanding of the site's local, urban and regional significance.[8] Prominent among its recommendations was the complete reworking of the inner-city roadway infrastructure for cars and trucks. Already at the center of suburban, regional and transcontinental railway networks, the site was to become the hub of a series of linked networks for rail, motorways, public transit and pedestrians. The structure was to be an integrated system that would order and serve the urban form at several levels underground, and at ground level, reinforcing its relationship with significant topographical features and urban figures such as Mont-Royal and the north–south axis of McGill College Avenue. Critical to all of this would be a representative public interior that was closely tied to and profoundly dependent on its connections to new urban transportation infrastructure.

Infrastructure served as the engine of development from the project's outset: the Canadian National Railway's suburban and national (transcontinental) lines constituted a starting point; the existing road infrastructure demanded resolution, so that the project would not be divided into isolated fragments; and the plan reinforced the notional need for an in-town motorway system that would feed directly into the project. The significance of the plan for the city, which envisaged the provision, all at once, of some 300,000m^2 of office space,[9] further relied on a series of parallel developments: the Canadian federal government's plans for an elevated urban motorway system linked to the regional and national network;[10] the City of Montreal's plans to proceed with the first line of the underground public transit metro system (opened in 1966); and the construction of the 1967 Universal Exposition or Expo 67, funded by Canada and the Quebec provincial government. The fortunes of each of these distinct plans were dependent upon the realization of the others. Each was incredibly ambitious in terms of its scale and speed of construction. Each was representative of a possible — even utopian — future for the city.

The elements anticipated and generated by the Ville-Marie plan constituted a complete and systematic overhaul of the city and its downtown, with the success of each component of the project again being contingent on that of the next. The plan, as realized, consisted of a core of three contiguous urban blocks: Place Ville-Marie (Henry N. Cobb, with the urban planner VIncent Ponte,

1955–62); the existing Central Station, Queen Elizabeth Hotel and offices for the Canadian National Railway (1942–60); and Place Bonaventure (Affleck Desbarats Dimakopoulos Lebensold Sise, 1967), supplemented by the Bonaventure metro station (Victor Prus, 1966). All of these at once connected to the city's downtown, its inner suburbs and its regional suburbs. The public interiors of the project were therefore the representative spaces for an urban citizen of the "new kind," one who typically lived and shopped in suburbs outside the center and who was conditioned by the representations and experiences of post-war consumer society. These citizens traveled to work in the city center by train and by car, in the latter instance directly through an elevated spur of the new raised motorway network that connected the project to the region and beyond.

The Character and Experience of New Spaces: The Public Interior
These same citizens — some 60,000 per day — disembarked directly into a new multi-level downtown core and extensive public interior that offered spatial arrangements and relationships that may have seemed completely new to the city but were familiar to the image-world of suburbia, whose representative interior was the shopping mall. Transported directly into the interior, large numbers of commuters and office workers moved through pedestrian concourses that were not merely functional or instrumental but represented a variety of instances of an urban public interior, each of which bore specific material and spatial attributes attached to those of the city.

Their appearances were abstract, yet drawn from European and American precedents that had been radically reworked. There were resonances with European arcades in the promenades of Place Ville-Marie,[11] with ancient Roman ruins in Bonaventure station, and with the Karnak Temple (among others) at Place Bonaventure. These associative aspects of the project's various appearances could also be found above ground. Place Ville-Marie's cruciform tower resembled the ideal Cartesian towers of Le Corbusier rendered in aluminum in the manner of Mies van der Rohe, while its public square was a modernist version of Francesco di Giorgio's Città Ideale. Place Bonaventure's fortified exterior evoked the forms of the Krak des Chevaliers castle, in concrete.

The two major constructions of the Ville-Marie project had quite different atmospheres. Place Ville-Marie, to the north, was both the site of greatest congestion and the representational center of the whole development: its public square at raised ground level was surrounded by representative commercial buildings and visually bound to the city's major topographic feature, Mont-Royal. Its interior promenade directly below was remarkably spacious despite its low and long proportions, which inferred a horizon and correspondingly horizontal movement. The measured facades of its shop fronts were similarly low, stopping just short of the ceiling. Backlit, sans serif lettering within the fascia unified all shops, while the space between fascia and ceiling was illuminated to make the whole space feel voluminous. At important crossings, signage was suspended from the ceiling, guiding people to connections and exits in the manner of an airport terminal. Daylight entered the promenade through four courtyards set into the square above.[12] The appearance of the promenade worked within and developed an orthodoxy that had emerged from the design of Victor Gruen's Southdale Center[13] and suggested an easy familiarity between the visual language of the corporate office lobby and that of the shopping mall; the money earned in the former spent in the latter.[14] The square above the Place Ville-Marie concourse was intended to be representative and civic in character, and accordingly was specially programmed for civic events throughout the year.[15] The architects hoped that this would become a genuine civic and political space, and on occasion it did indeed become the scene of political rallies and, notably, political protest.[16]

above: Place Ville-Marie, Montreal. Architects I.M. Pei & Associates. Photo George Cserna photographs and papers, 1937–1978, Avery Architectural & Fine Arts Library © Columbia University in the City of New York

To the south, Place Bonaventure had spatial and material characteristics quite distinct from those of Place Ville-Marie. Its huge building was a monumental structure in its own right, accommodating a mix of functions and facilities in a deep-plan block with concrete walls designed like battlements.[17] Its variety of interiors followed, or led, the specific characteristics of its stack of apparently incongruous contents, from railway lines at the very bottom, to a shopping concourse and passages, motorway entrance, bus terminal, exhibition and trade halls, conference center and rooftop hotel. Writing in the mid-1970s, Reyner Banham described Montreal as the first "mega-city" and Place Bonaventure as a true megastructure.[18] Within it, a visitor had the impression of moving through a kind of ruin set on a rocky landscape. The pedestrian concourse, lined with shops and restaurants, featured stepped floor surfaces that wound through the field of slab-like columns, evoking the coarse landscape of granite upon which the city is built. Spaces like the trade halls above offered the image of the vast halls of an ancient Egyptian temple.[19] As one moved up through the structure, one always had the sense of traversing different scenes, or realms. This impression of "travel" across different terrains and even historical periods was consistent with the experience of movement across the project as a whole, and reinforced by the design of Bonaventure metro station.

above and right: Bonaventure station, Montreal.
Architect Victor Prus. Prus's design set the
tone for the entire metro network: the spaces
of infrastructure were to be significant and
representative public interiors for the broad
public who experienced them every day. Photos
Mark Pimlott, courtesy of the author

Bonaventure Station

The first phase of the underground metro public transit network
was completed in 1966. Like all such infrastructure, its effect on the
city's sense of space was profound. Though plans for mass transit
networks had been laid since the late nineteenth century, this was the
first to be realized. The system was designed following the methods
of the Paris metro in some memorable aspects, notably in its use
of rubber-wheeled train carriages.[20] This mark of Parisian character
was directed towards Montreal's distinctly francophone reality, while
allusions to metropolitan conditions beyond the continent chimed
with Montreal's desire to position itself internationally, a desire it
had declared quite openly with its bid for the Universal Exposition.[21]
Montreal's mayor, Jean Drapeau, sought to make it the most modern
city, an ambition grounded in its historical significance as the largest
trading city in North America up to the middle of the nineteenth
century. The new metro, then, bore the burden of several ambitions,
reflected in the total design of the entire system, from the palette
of materials and their details[22] to the integration of signage and
wayfinding systems. The materials of the city streets were reprised in
the materials the metro was made of.[23]

The metro stations were accordingly designed as though they
were underground monuments. Bonaventure station took the
form of a series of connected vaulted chambers three levels deep,
with connections to Place Bonaventure to the north and Windsor

station to the west. The space evoked ruins, specifically the Baths of Caracalla and the *carceri* of Giambattista Piranesi. When the station's architect, Victor Prus, wrote of making the Montreal metro an extension of the street, he may have held an ideal image of the city as one that contained such monuments. The station's spaces created new hierarchies within the city's public interiors, whose protagonists until that moment were the department stores on rue Ste-Catherine, the Mount Royal Hotel, the Dominion Square building, Windsor station, the banks in rue Saint-Jacques, the Forum, Central Station and the newly added Place Bonaventure and Place Ville-Marie.[24] Prus's design set the tone for the entire metro network: the spaces of infrastructure were to be significant and representative public interiors for the broad public who experienced them every day. With this critical addition, all of the spaces of the extended ville intérieure — from the modest to the grandiose — would contain all of the hierarchies one might expect within a traditional European city.

A Utopian City: The Effect of Expo 67

The public interiors of the ville intérieure were propositional in that they generated a new image for the city tied to its landscape, material culture and desired associations, among them a modernity expressed through technology, mobility and corporate labor. One aspect of this image was tied to a future that had already been realized in the present. Specifically, the future embodied within the ville intérieure was reinforced by the anticipation — and then experience — of the Universal Exposition, which offered itself as a new utopian city on the river, within view and easy reach of the real city. Constructed over the same period and just as quickly as the elevated motorway system, the metro, Place Bonaventure and the final stage of Place Ville-Marie, it presented a parallel to the spaces of the ville intérieure and confirmed the popular impression that the city's future had arrived in all its fullness and all at once. Expo 67 is remembered primarily for singular buildings that graced its glorious summer: R. Buckminster Fuller's US pavilion,[25] Frei Otto's West German pavilion — and, of course, Moshe Safdie's famous Habitat 67, which still stands today.[26] Pavilions that exposed the great humanist theme of the exhibition, Man and His World (Terre des hommes), were similarly experimental environments: the Man the Producer and Man the Explorer pavilions, by the architects of Place Bonaventure, featured gargantuan cor-ten space frames on a three-dimensional hexagonal grid. These, the national pavilions, and those dedicated to industry used innovative displays for didactic purposes, often consciously directed towards the young.[27]

Expo's menagerie of experimental and exotic architecture was tied together by an elaborate system of infrastructure dedicated to transport and communication, the means by which its nearly 60 million visitors actually used the utopian city. The metro traveled directly to Île Sainte-Hélène; a new train, the Expo Express, departed from the new Cité du Havre to traverse a new bridge over the river to Île Nôtre-Dame. From their points of arrival, visitors could take either of two forms of elevated minirail, or strike out onto the pedestrian street system under their own power or aided by *pédicab*, a bicycle taxi. The footpaths linked the pavilions, which were interspersed with canals and other lagoons around which various forms of entertainment played. The citizens of this fledgling utopia could sit on newly designed benches under the reflected light of a new street-illumination system or make telephone calls under plastic hemispheres. All was new, experimental and hopeful — and all, apparently, the product of the partnership of technology and humanism. Expo 67 was a plausible demonstration of an entire "working city" whose lessons were also echoed within the new spaces and systems of the "real city." This had a significant impact on the popular reception of the ville intérieure and the perception of its possible freedoms. The attitude that the public assumed at the exhibition was transferred to, and thereafter felt across, the interior network as it grew beyond the multi-level downtown core.

Expo 67 Montreal. **left:** Canada Pavilion. Architects Ashworth, Robbie, Vaughan & Williams; Schoeier & Barkham; A. Matthew Stankiewicz. **right:** US Pavilion. Architect R. Buckminster Fuller, Cambridge Seven Associates. From Robert Fulford, photographers John de Visser, Peter Varley, Harold Whyte, Remember Expo: A Pictorial Record (Toronto: McLalland and Stewart, 1968)

The Multi-level Core as Part of a Total Plan

Expo 67 not only presented a working system complete with compelling representative figures, it offered a complete scenography that fused landscape, architecture, infrastructure and technology. The ville intérieure plan as imagined by Vincent Ponte was intended to similarly offer a complete urban scenography that fused infrastructure, architecture and representative landscape into one three-dimensional structure that could expand beyond the new core. He wished to integrate the below-ground structures of the Ville-Marie development with those above ground. And, just as there was a hierarchy to the underground network — an aspect indebted to the representational public interior of Victor Prus's Metro Bonaventure — there was to be a hierarchical arrangement of spaces above ground too. Alongside his principle of incremental, ad hoc extension of the underground interior network, Ponte adhered to precepts of Baroque city planning and meaningful relationships between buildings and their geographic and topological settings. In the case of Montreal, the axis that led from Central Station to Mont-Royal along McGill College Avenue was to become the device that revealed the "meaning" of Pei, Cobb and Ponte's master plan and the three-dimensional downtown within the structures both below and above ground.[28] The ville intérieure was, in this way, designed to be a complete and three-dimensional construction of urban interiority — a condition of interior that was not limited to the spaces beneath the streets or the self-imposed constraints of a megastructure.

Connective Tissue and Ad Hoc Extension

Following the first phase of its construction in 1962, the project's public interior — the core of the ville intérieure — was almost immediately supplemented by a series of informal extensions, connections and links to separate developments. All together, these generated an underground pedestrian network linked to other large-scale structures; at first, largely office buildings. From these beginnings, new kinds of interior realms accumulated, aggregated to the burgeoning network, many of which found their inspiration in the structures and infrastructure at the heart of the downtown core. First as part of I.M. Pei & Associates' team, and later as an independent urban planner, Vincent Ponte was most responsible for the principle on which the entire ville intérieure grew: one of incremental, ad hoc accretion, with the driving idea of extension until the point of "completion" in a circular interior route around the downtown. With the City of Montreal offering benefits to developments that would include underground connections to the network, a possible link to the subway systems encouraged the construction of a passage. Small retail units would then emerge where there were enough passersby and, almost naturally, the passage would be seen as one with those facilities that attended the metro, wherein an atmosphere of informality fostered natural hierarchies of space. The development principle of connectivity to the metro and the benefits of incorporating underground links yielded an underground network that, increasingly, was consciously planned.

The ville intérieure has gradually unfolded as a vast space that accommodates a very wide variety of programs, from the most modest to the most expansive commercial activities, from simple tunnels to concourses and large public interiors, buildings and facilities, within which a kind of typological familiarity has ensued. A completely naturalized aspect of the city's landscape, it owes its existence to a plan, to a series of simultaneous large-scale infrastructural developments, to the principle of ad hoc extension, and to an atmosphere of hope, with all its concomitant freedoms, that prevailed throughout much of the 1960s.

below: The extended ville intérieure today: Complexe Desjardins shopping mall. Photo David Thompson/Media Bakery

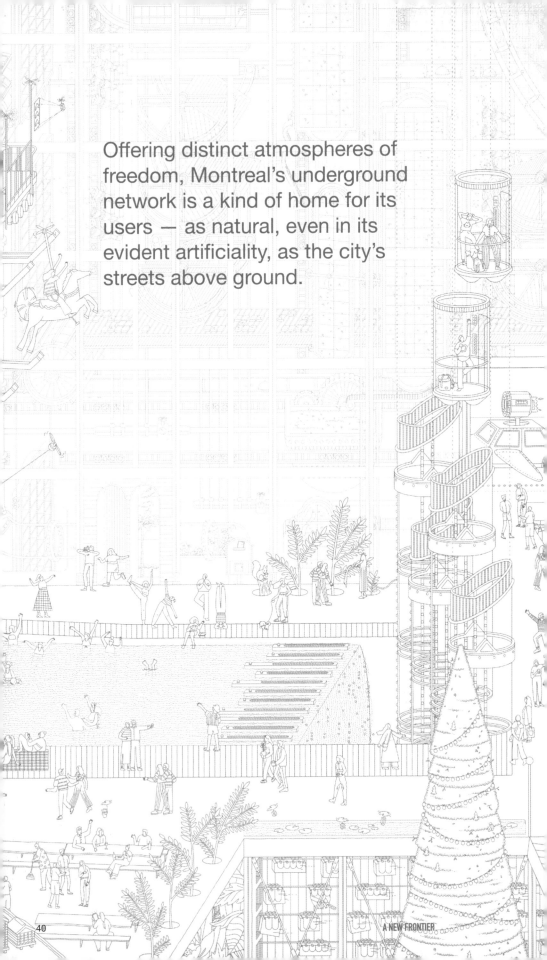

Offering distinct atmospheres of freedom, Montreal's underground network is a kind of home for its users — as natural, even in its evident artificiality, as the city's streets above ground.

HELSINKI: CITY OF DEEP COLLABORATIONS

Ilkka Vähäaho, City of Helsinki

With an urban grain that is compact, more medium-scale than towering, Helsinki is a city that uses its multi-layered underground in a highly effective way. Underground resources are reserved mainly for uses that are for the common good. This means places where people can gather, as well as utilities such as the city's 1,350km district heating and cooling network, which recycles energy from local sources that would otherwise go to waste.

Temppeliaukio Church, Helsinki, 1960–69. Architects Timo and Tuomo Suomalainen. In Helsinki, the technical process of construction has generated its own aesthetics, with the rough rock walls expressing a certain power and stability as well as a connection with nature. Photo Lingxiao Xie via Getty Images

Reserved routes for new tunnels

Reserved for future UG spaces

Existing tunnels and UG spaces

Reserved for future use (not designated)

Rock surface less than 10m from ground level

An ethos of cooperation defines the City of Helsinki's relations with the numerous partners involved in the making of underground space: its planning, financing, design, construction and maintenance. And the connective tissue of the underground extends far beyond the city itself, with a visionary plan to link Helsinki with its sister city, Tallinn, the capital of Estonia, via an 80km subsea tunnel across the Gulf of Finland.

Finland began constructing its huge network of underground facilities in the 1980s. Today, the Finnish capital has some 400 separate underground facilities and tunnels, the deepest about 100m below sea level. Around 90 of these spaces are dual-purpose, designed to meet normal needs with strengthening just for exceptional times. If required, 72 hours are enough to turn a sporting field into a shelter — to install decontamination showers and toilets, and then shut the doors tight.

Impetus for Underground Development

Low-lying, watery, Helsinki covers 214km^2 of land and 500km^2 of sea. Home to 1.5 million people, around a quarter of Finland's population, the Greater Helsinki area is the world's northernmost city of this scale, though winters are tempered by the influence of the Gulf Stream, with the January/February average hovering around –5C. Escaping a severe winter climate is therefore not a primary consideration for underground development, as it is in Montreal. Instead, the main drivers are the favorable characteristics of the bedrock and the fact that Finns are used to having lots of open space around them, even in urban areas. As the city structure is becoming denser, more facilities suited for different purposes are being placed underground. Another reason for going underground is seismic risk. While earth tremors in Finland are usually less than a magnitude of three, underground solutions reduce their effects even more.

Master Plan

With the growth in underground construction and planning, and the need to coordinate different projects, the City of Helsinki took its first steps towards preparing a master plan for its entire network of underground facilities in the early 2000s. Although the city has maintained an underground space allocation plan since the 1980s, this more comprehensive general plan, with its legally binding status, reinforces the systematic nature and quality of underground construction and the exchange of information related to it. The

> " In simple terms, underground facilities can be thought of as providing the ultimate 'green roof.' Facilities placed fully underground do not impact the surface aesthetic (once constructed) and can leave space for natural ground surfaces and flora that maintain the natural ecological exchanges of thermal radiation, convection and moisture exchange. "

underground master plan (UMP) allows control over the location of significant new underground rock facilities and traffic tunnels and their interconnections.[1] It includes space allocations for transport, emergency shelters, sports, various installations and establishments, water and energy supply, parking, storage, waste management and other similar facilities. The aim is to achieve joint use wherever possible, for example with a multi-purpose tunnel network or shared parking.

The UMP is administered by the City of Helsinki Urban Environment Division (formerly known as the Helsinki City Planning Department). The City of Helsinki Soil and Bedrock Unit GEO[2] has defined the areas and elevation levels that are suitable for the construction of large, hall-like spaces. These underground resources play a central role in the development of the urban fabric of Helsinki and the adjoining areas, helping to create a more unified and eco-efficient structure. "In simple terms, underground facilities can be thought of as providing the ultimate 'green roof.' Facilities placed fully underground do not impact the surface aesthetic (once constructed) and can leave space for natural ground surfaces and flora that maintain the natural ecological exchanges of thermal radiation, convection and moisture exchange."[3]

Construction

The expansion of Helsinki's subsurface has been aided by the quality of the bedrock, consisting mainly of old Precambrian rocks, which for the most part are ideal for tunneling and building underground spaces.[4] There are no sedimentary rocks in the Helsinki area, although there are several fracture zones formed by rock block movements that cross the bedrock in the city center.[5]

The average price of tunnels and underground spaces in Finland is €100 per cubic meter, including excavation, rock reinforcement, grouting and underdrainage — which is significantly lower than in

below: Extract from rock surface model, showing estimated rock surface based on bedrock confirmation drillings. Image City of Helsinki Real Estate Department

many other places, and around one-tenth of the engineering cost of creating caverns in Hong Kong, for example. To date, only the drill and blast (D&B) method has been used for rock excavations; Tunnel Boring Machines (TBMs) have not yet proven competitive in the hard rock conditions of Finland.

However, it is not only effective D&B technology and extensive experience working in urban areas that keeps the cost of tunneling so low. Since the rock materials are excellent, there is no need to use cast concrete lining, which can increase costs by up to 200 percent. Rock-mechanics engineers dimension the underground space as a rock-framed, self-supporting structure and the outcome is not only cheaper than a space with a concreted arch support but also — in the opinion of the author of this text, at least — far more beautiful.

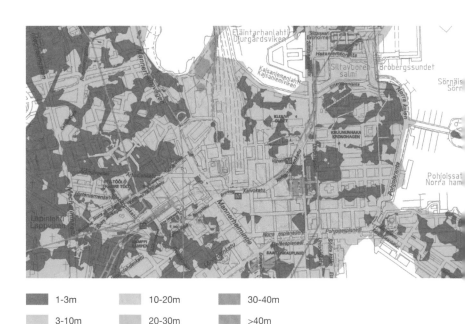

▓ 1-3m	░ 10-20m	▓ 30-40m
░ 3-10m	▒ 20-30m	▓ >40m

above: Interior view of Tempelliaukio Church, Helsinki, 1960–69. Architects Timo and Tuomo Suomalainen. Photo Hou via Getty Images

Aesthetics

The technical process of construction has generated its own aesthetics, as exemplified in an early project, Temppeliaukio Church (1960–69), where the rough rock walls express a certain power and stability as well as a connection with nature. The architects were two brothers, Timo and Tuomo Suomalainen, who as teenagers had already gained first-hand experience in drilling and even blasting rock when building a new home in Hamina, on a plot given to their evacuee family in 1944.[6] The shades of granite in the church walls — red, purple and gray — determined the color scheme of the interiors. The metals were also chosen to match the colors of the stone — steel, made bluish by hammering, and non-oxidized copper for the front facing of the gallery and cupola.

Another iconic project is the underground swimming pool in Itäkeskus by Arkkitehtitoimisto HKP (1993). Quarried out of solid rock, it has pools, gyms and a fitness center over two floors and can accommodate around 1,000 visitors at a time (some 400,000 people use it every year). If the need arises, the hall can be converted into an

above: Aerial view of Temppeliaukio Church, Helsinki, 1960–69. Architects Timo and Tuomo Suomalainen. Photo Hannu Vallas/Alamy.com/Argusphoto

below: Underground
swimming pool in Itäkeskus,
1993. Quarried out of solid
rock, the swimming hall
can be converted to an
emergency shelter for 3,800
people if required. Architects
Arkkitehtitoimisto HKP. Photo
Olli Häkämies, courtesy of City
of Helsinki Media Bank

above: Dramatic lighting is a
feature of Tapiola Central Parking,
2016. Architects Arkkitehtitoimisto
HKP Oy. Photo Kari Palsila,
courtesy of the architects

emergency shelter for 3,800 people. The architects of the swimming pool are also the designers of Tapiola Central Parking (2016), with its striking lighting scheme.

More attention than ever is being paid to the attractiveness of underground spaces. For the inhabitants of Helsinki, these are not simply places of transit, to be hurried through, but places for eating, drinking, sports, dancing, visiting the theater, target shooting and kart racing, among many other pursuits.

Maximizing the use of land resources is something that is seen at the scale of infrastructure, too. The subsurface of Katri Vala Park, for example, houses four totally independent utilities — storage rooms, a heat pump station, a utility tunnel and a tunnel for cleaned wastewater — and the possibility of building one more space between the existing underground "floors" is currently being investigated.

Dealing with Water Services as Part of Underground Infrastructure

Helsinki has been building all-in-one utility tunnels since 1977. These now extend over 300km, accommodating transmission lines and pipes for district heating and cooling, electricity and water supply systems, as well as a large number of different cable links. The preliminary and construction phase planning required for the rock construction of the utility tunnels is primarily the responsibility of the Helsinki GEO. Facilities designed by GEO include tunnel lines, halls, vertical shafts and the necessary access tunnels.[7]

Raw water for the Helsinki region comes from Lake Päijänne via a 120km rock tunnel that runs on average 40m below ground. The water requires few processing steps before use, thanks to the good quality of the water reserves and the constant low temperature and secure environment during transport.

Wastewater treatment is carried out centrally at the Viikinmäki underground plant, the largest in the Nordic countries based on the load: the average flow is 280,000m^3 per day, while the peak flow is 700,000m^3. In operation since 1994, the plant replaced a dozen smaller treatment plants, all of them above ground, allowing these sites to be zoned for more valuable uses.

The plant processes both industrial wastewater (about 15 percent of its load) and domestic wastewater from 870,000 people in the Helsinki region. The wastewater is treated mechanically, chemically and biologically at the activated sludge plant: the sludge separated from the wastewater is then treated in underground digesters, and the biogas generated in the digestion process is used to produce heat and electricity — the wastewater treatment plant is 100 percent self-sufficient in heat and in 2018 reached 97 percent self-sufficiency in electrical energy. At the end of the process, the dried and digested sludge is turned into garden soil in the composting field, while treated wastewater is fed through a 16km underground discharge tunnel into the sea, sufficiently far from the coastline.[8]

However, Helsinki's growing population and the changes brought by global warming present new challenges, as the amount of wastewater and extreme climate phenomena increase. Since there is no scope to expand the underground plant in the same Viikinmäki hill area, bold and innovative ideas will be required to develop its wastewater treatment processes to meet increasingly strict regulations.

A Carbon-neutral City

The City of Helsinki is preparing to be carbon neutral by 2035. As one step in this shift away from fossil fuels, the energy company, Helen Oy, is converting artificial rock caverns to store warm water connected to district heating. The caves, located in the Mustikkamaa recreational island of Helsinki,[9] will be filled with 260,000m³ of tap water, kept at maximum 90C through a district heating connection from Helen Oy's heat production processes. The heat stored in the water will be released into the district heating network with heat exchangers. The full energy storage capacity of the caves — 120 megawatt hours — is enough to provide for half of Helsinki's summer-time district heat consumption (mainly domestic hot water) for four days. It can also be used in winter to ease peak demand that would otherwise require extra generation in coal- and oil-fired processes. Because the heat does not have to be produced as it is consumed, heat energy storage will compensate for the higher fluctuations in the availability and cost of renewable energy.

Mustikkamaa's subterranean hot water lakes will be similar to the subterranean cold water reservoirs used in Helsinki's district cooling network. Two caves built into the bedrock — one under the downtown Esplanade Park (capacity 25,000m³), the other in Pasila (11,000m³) — are integrated with heat pumps, which work with the cooling network to produce district heat by recycling energy. As cold water circulates in the network, releasing its cooling energy, the heat pumps recover heat from diverse available sources, including treated wastewater and data centers, and feed it back into the district heating network. The fundamental idea of district heating and cooling is to use local resources that would otherwise be wasted. With district heating, pavements and passages can also be kept clear in the winter with an energy-efficient snow-melting system.

Helen Oy has plans for more energy storage, investigating the potential to build the world's first seasonal heat storage facility in former fuel oil caverns (constructed by Shell Oil in the 1970s) in the new ecological suburb of Kruunuvuorenranta. The caves would be filled in summer with sun-warmed seawater at around 20C and used in winter as a source for heat pumps to produce district heating water at over 80C. Helsinki's district heating and cooling system now serves the majority of the city's homes (around 90 percent of demand). Extending over 1,350km, and expanding at a rate of 15km to 20km a year, it is the fastest-growing network in Europe.

Everything is Recycled: A Second Life for Obsolete Spaces
Some 450km north of Helsinki, the Callio program is finding new uses for another kind of underground space that has outlived its original purpose: the copper and zinc mine at Pyhäjärvi, commissioned in the 1960s. An elevator takes just three minutes to descend 1,400m to the main underground facilities — a network of spacious tunnels, rooms with modern LED lighting, cozy social and dining areas, and even a sauna.[10] The opening up of the mine began before its decommissioning. Already it has hosted dance performances and the world's deepest concert (at 1,271m). Its 11km, spiraling main

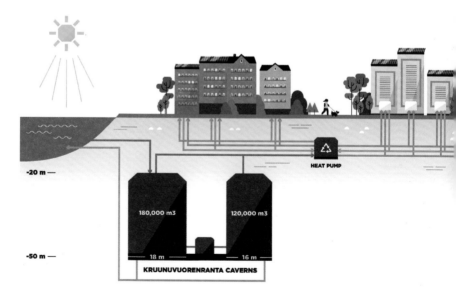

above: Obsolete oil reservoirs located 3km from the center of Helsinki will be adapted to use seawater heated by the sun and integrated into the energy system of an ecological suburb. Image Helen Oy

Son et lumière show at the cold water reservoir for district cooling in Helsinki's city center.
Photo Helen Oy

access tunnel is used for uphill running and cycling events. With the end of mining, these facilities will become part of a multidisciplinary operating environment. The mine has four existing environmentally controlled underground laboratories — past projects include cosmic-ray experiments. Proposed new uses, both scientific and commercial, include a secure data center, pumped hydroelectric energy storage, insect and fish farming and underground greenhouses. Cultivation tests (for mushrooms, potatoes, hops) are currently being carried out at a depth of 660m. Here, close to the Arctic Circle, there could be five subterranean summers a year.

A Long-term Vision
Since excavating bedrock is a one-off action and the spaces it carves out endure, there has to be a long-term vision governing their use. When planning new construction, it is important to reserve sufficient space for the future provision of public utilities, such as tunnels and shafts for traffic and technical maintenance. Likewise, the valuable subterranean space must be exploited in a practical way, without wasting any future resources.

The City of Helsinki has reserved areas for the construction of as yet unclassified underground facilities, with the aim of reducing the pressures on underground resources in the city center. The suitability of rock areas for different purposes will be studied when preparing urban plans. There are now some 40 unnamed rock resource reservations without a designated purpose, covering a total area of almost 14km^2 (or 6.4 percent of the land mass of Helsinki). The selection of unclassified resources is both rock resource and purpose driven, as the survey takes account of their accessibility, the present and planned ground-level uses of these areas, traffic connections, land ownership and possible recreational, landscape and environmental protection values.

Real estate owners may restrict the use of the space under their lot or get compensation only if the proposed use is harmful or causes some financial loss. Finnish legislation is not precise about the extent of land ownership — neither above nor below ground. But it does distinguish between the right to use property and the ownership of land. The lower boundary of the right to use property is limited to the depth where it can be technically utilized, which usually means a depth of 6m — a practical measure for building one or, at the most, two basement levels. This 6m limit is the normal practice, though is not enshrined in Finnish law. If landowners want to add multiple underground levels to their buildings, they must have a building permit. Equally, the right to build a deep cellar must be in accordance with zoning. The question is not one of land ownership, but of the right to use land for building purposes. This is mainly controlled by master planning, by zoning (town planning), and ultimately by building permits.

Talsinki: A Pragmatic Utopia

In 2008 an international ideas competition was organized to imagine the future of the city. The winner of "Greater Helsinki Vision 2050" proposed an 80km subsea tunnel crossing the Gulf of Finland to connect the Finnish capital with Tallinn, the capital of Estonia. That vision of a fixed link could soon be realized. Helsinki and Tallinn enjoy close cultural and economic ties. Both metropolitan areas have grown enormously over the last 20 years, and since Estonia joined the European Union in 2004 it has been able to apply for joint funding for EU projects. More than nine million people take the ferry between the two cities annually. The journey typically takes around two and a half hours; a high-speed rail link via the subsea tunnel would cut that time to only 30 minutes.

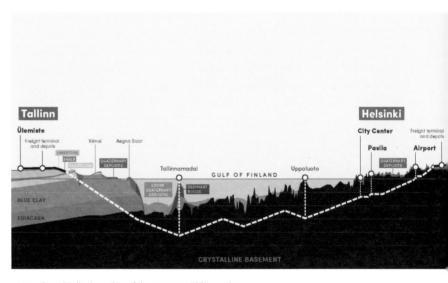

above: Longitudinal section of the proposed 80km subsea tunnel connecting the capitals of Finland and Estonia.
Image Muotoilutoimisto Kairo Oy

A pre-feasibility study done in 2015 determined that the rail tunnel, with an estimated construction cost of €15 billion, would be economically viable. The City of Helsinki has collaborated with the Geological Surveys of Finland and Estonia in a study of the geological and geotechnical properties of the proposed route of the tunnel, which is located on the boundary between the Fennoscandian Shield and the East European Platform. In the Helsinki area, the exposed old Precambrian hard bedrock is overlaid with a thin layer of loose Quaternary sediments. Near Tallinn, the old crystalline basement meets younger sedimentary rocks. Limited experience of tunneling in the conditions near the interface between these two formations will make the project challenging, especially at its southern end. The possible methods for tunneling are D&B techniques, suited to the hard rock conditions in Finland, and the use of TBMs as an alternative

below: Map of Helsinki. Areas in green are owned by the City of Helsinki; white-colored areas are owned by others. Image City of Helsinki, Land Property Development and Plots

at the Estonian site. After financial negotiations and project planning, construction could start in 2025 at the earliest, with the tunnel being operational in the 2030s.[11] The Helsinki–Tallinn twin city already has a new, unofficial, name: "Talsinki."

At the other end of the Baltic Sea, another twinning of cities provides immediate proof of the benefits of greater integration. Before the Øresund Bridge opened in 2000, Malmö was a declining manufacturing center and Copenhagen was a significantly wealthier region. The opening of the bridge not only reduced the physical distance between them to 16km, or a 15-minute commute, but also brought them closer together culturally and economically.

These qualities of openness and close cooperation also define the City of Helsinki's relations with the numerous partners involved in the planning, financing, construction and maintenance of underground space. As many of these collaborations are carried out informally, trust between the parties is essential, particularly when developing processes and sharing risks. Here, again, we see the benefits of greater integration and holistic planning. The city-owned Helen Oy is one of the largest energy companies in Finland, producing electricity and district heating and cooling. Water services and waste management are supplied by a municipal body, the Helsinki Region Environmental Services Authority HSY. In addition, the city now owns some 63 percent of the land area of Helsinki, having acquired land with a long-term and goal-oriented focus since the early 1900s. Planning for the long term means, among other things, publishing a climate roadmap that sets out how Helsinki will become a climate-resilient city by 2050. It means building more housing for a growing population while keeping the urban fabric compact and at a human scale. It also means an open-minded approach to the use — and potential adaptation or re-use — of the subsurface of the city.

The United Nations ranks Finland as the "world's happiest country." According to the UN report, the quality of people's lives can be validly assessed by a variety of subjective measures of well-being. It notes that "the large international differences in life evaluations are driven by the differences in how people connect with each other and with their shared institutions and social norms."[12] In Helsinki, as in other cities in Finland, the use of the underground increases the sense of well-being in multiple ways, helping people connect with each other and providing shared facilities that contribute to a feeling of personal security in a fast-changing world.

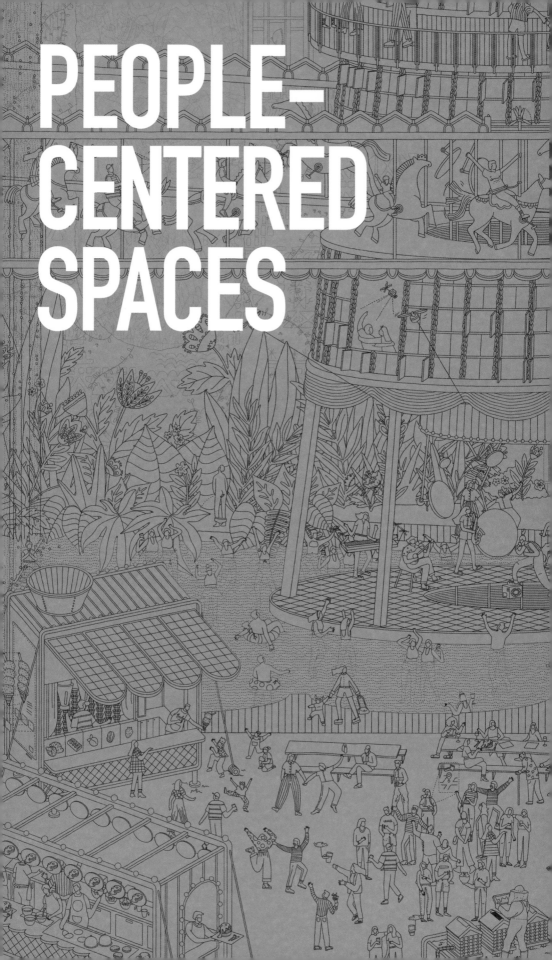

PEOPLE-CENTERED SPACES

Understanding how to make people feel comfortable in underground space is key to getting this largely untapped resource accepted as a natural extension of the city. "People-centered Spaces" presents an eclectic selection of buildings and projects with concepts that challenge even the most deep-rooted prejudices against the underground. Exploring how to integrate the elements of light, air and vegetation, they create new kinds of subterranean spaces that foster a vital sense of connection with the wider world.

THE RESILIENT CITY

Will Symons, AECOM

As cities reached upward in the nineteenth and twentieth centuries, they also extended downward, creating the substructure on which their prosperity now rests. New York, Hong Kong, Singapore, London, Moscow, Paris — indeed, any modern city — would be unimaginable without its subterranean networks carrying flows of communication, people, goods, energy and water.

The Body of the City

Perhaps more than any other system, cities rely on their underground rail networks for their economic well-being — these are the arteries that supply their lifeblood, connecting work and home, providing access to the oxygen of creativity, cultural events and domesticity while relieving congestion and pollution on the surface. In turn, the complex web of receptacles and pipes that store, treat and reticulate water, the supply chains that provide sustenance, and the wastewater systems that collect, treat and dispose of the resulting excreta, are the city's alimentary system. The uninterruptable copper and fiber-optic cables that travel in conduits under our feet enable an equally critical human need — to communicate and cohere, forming the city's sensitive nervous systems. Finally, the muscles of this urban body are the production and distribution networks which create and then transfer energy to the metropolis from its rural hinterlands, providing thermal comfort, lighting our way and helping to supply all the services we associate with modern life. Without these energetic muscles, the city would atrophy.

In many ways, the historical use of subterranean spaces is the history of modern cities. However cities today are facing an increasingly uncertain and disruptive future. Continued rapid urbanization and

population growth are placing immense strain on existing urban systems and services. Extreme weather events are becoming more frequent and severe as a result of climate change; heat and drought, together with rising sea levels, are multiplying the stressors on both people and infrastructure. To meet these challenges, we need to reimagine the built form that has successfully supported urban life over the past two centuries. Here again, the underground has a critical role to play. By radically expanding the possibilities for its use and combining the latest technology with age-old knowledge, we can make the body of our cities more resilient.

The Sheltering Underground

Different cities develop their underground in different ways. In some places these systems are government-owned and operated, and in others they exist entirely in the private sector and are exposed to the vagaries of the market. Many are a mixture of both. But regardless of how it is funded, much of the infrastructure that is currently being built will need to support the success of communities for generations to come. In the case of a rapidly growing city that is already exposed to the impacts of increasing urban heat, this means making better use of the capacity of underground spaces to maintain remarkably stable temperatures due to earth's ability to absorb and store heat. Rather than being just a tube for trains, a new metro rail tunnel should provide a cool place of refuge, ventilated not only mechanically but by natural means. For workers evacuated from their office due to a power failure on a 46C day — as happened in Melbourne on 7 February 2009 — having an accessible metro tunnel to shelter in, with piped drinking water and medical supplies on hand, could mean the difference between life and death.

Derinkuyu is one of 22 large-scale underground cities carved out of the soft tufa rock of Central Anatolia over a period of 1,500 years. Individual homes within the complex were focused around a large multi-functional space, excavated and enlarged over generations. Photo Pakhnyushchy/Shutterstock.com

Heat is a silent and largely invisible killer — vulnerable people die from its effects in their homes and hospital emergency rooms. And although heat degrades infrastructure, the urban fabric is not dramatically destroyed as it is with other kinds of natural disasters. In the US, extreme heat kills more people every year than any other type of weather-related event. More than 2,300 people died in India during a 2015 heatwave, and a year later the town of Phalodi in Jodhpur reached 51C, the highest temperature ever recorded in the country. Extreme heat events are becoming longer and more intense, and increasing urban density means that more people are being exposed. C40 Cities, a network of the world's megacities committed to addressing climate change, predicts that by 2050 around 1.6 billion people in 970 cities around the world will experience average summertime maximum temperatures above 35C. Artificially cooling spaces to shelter people from these temperatures is expensive and in countries reliant on fossil fuels it exacerbates the climate change that is driving the extreme heat.

The idea of metro tunnels doubling as climate shelters is one way that our underground infrastructure could have a greater degree of built-in flexibility, making it more responsive to advances in technology and a range of human needs. This kind of adaptation to the conditions of everyday life is something we see in many historical examples of underground use, including the farmers' cave dwellings (yáodòng) in the Loess Plateau in northwest China, and perhaps most notably the subterranean cities of Cappadocia in Central Anatolia, Turkey. In a volcanic landscape shaped by the erosion of wind and floodwaters, 22 large-scale cities were carved out of the soft tufa rock over a period of more than 1,500 years. The largest of these is Kaymakli, which housed nearly 60,000 people at its peak. The deepest is Derinkuyu, which in some places extends down five stories or 90m.

In a region regularly exposed to foreign invasions, Derinkuyu could shelter 20,000 people. Connections were made through hidden passages behind above-ground homes, and each level could be independently secured from within. There was also an 8km underground connection to another subterranean city nearby. In addition to being naturally defensible, the underground spaces

above: Cappadocia cave houses.
Photo Apurva Madia/Alamy.com/Argusphoto

were also more resistant to earthquakes. Summers in Cappadocia are hot and dry, while winters bring deep snow. All year round the underground caverns' temperature remains a stable 13C. Combined with a low-humidity environment, this allowed the inhabitants of Derinkuyu to store fresh fruit and vegetables for many months, evening out seasonal fluctuations in their food supply. (The caverns are still used today to store thousands of tons of fresh produce.) Fresh air was brought in through 52 ventilation chimneys, some of them up to 80m high. Redundancy was built into both the ventilation system and the water supply, providing back up if any single supply point failed or was contaminated. Besides storage for food and weapons, the multi-level complex of interconnected tunnels and rooms contained wells, oil and wine presses, a vast bathhouse complete with a set of private rooms and tall ceilings to let the steam rise, churches, schools, tombs and even stables for domestic animals. Individual homes within the complex were focused around a large multi-functional space, excavated and enlarged over generations — a place for eating, sitting and sleeping, decorated with carpets, pillows and blankets. This was a naturally climate-controlled city that provided its inhabitants with the means to survive and thrive, living in harmony with nature.

above: Coober Pedy, Australia. Underground billiards room at Radeka's Downunder Underground Motel. Photo Andrew Watson/Lonely Planet Images via Getty Images

left: Coober Pedy, Australia. Serbian Orthodox Church of Saint Elijah the Prophet. The church lies 17m below ground level and was constructed in 1993. Photo Quinn Rooney/Getty Images News via Getty Images

With average summer temperatures above 35C and regularly exceeding 45C, Coober Pedy in the harsh outback of northern South Australia could be seen as a modern-day Derinkuyu. Although the region has been inhabited by the Antakirinja Matu-Yankunytjatjara Aboriginal people for more than 40,000 years, the present town of 1,800 people was settled by European opal miners in 1915. While digging an estimated 250,000 mine shafts, these settlers also dug into the earth to provide shelter, including houses, churches, motels and shops. Here, the cost of constructing an underground three-bedroom house is roughly equivalent to an above-ground house of the same size — the spaces are light-filled and roomy, and the natural chilling ability of the surrounding soil dramatically reduces cooling bills. Learning from communities like Coober Pedy and scaling up these methods in cities around the world would increase the equity of access to cool spaces, dramatically increase the survivability of urban areas during heatwaves, and significantly reduce the cost of providing thermal comfort.

above: The sixth-century Basilica Cistern (left) is one of several hundred ancient cisterns that lie beneath Istanbul. Photo Sergey Dzyuba/Alamy.com/Argusphoto; Tokyo's G-Cans project (right), completed in 2009, is the world's largest underground floodwater diversion facility. Photo John S. Lander via Getty Images

right: The water square in Benthemplein, Rotterdam channels rainwater into a series of three basins of increasing depth, with the deepest basin only filling after a prolonged downpour. Architects Urbanisten NL. Photo courtesy of the architects

Living with Water

Climate change means that many of our cities must contend with rising sea levels and more frequent episodes of intense precipitation at the same time as adapting to lower average annual rates of rainfall. Yet water, and more specifically its erratic supply, has been an issue ever since people first came together to form settlements, and one that has been resolved in ingenious and sometimes beautiful ways. One striking example of this is the 1,400-year-old Basilica Cistern, built to supply the Great Palace of Constantinople (in today's Istanbul) with water brought from the Belgrade Forest 15km away. A water filtration system with a capacity of 100 million liters, it is also a cathedral-like space with a vaulted roof supported by more than 300 intricately carved marble and granite columns. The same marrying of beauty and utility, of form and function, is also possible in modern infrastructure. In Tokyo, the G-Cans facility — a surge tank for stormwater — is another impressive cathedral-like space, this time rendered in concrete.

In the Netherlands, many parts of Rotterdam now experience regular flooding and the municipal administration has for some years promoted the construction of underground tanks to collect and hold the excess rainwater. These structures are expensive, however, and since they are usually hidden, taxpayers do not understand how effective they are. The city has therefore adopted a strategy of connecting new water storage systems with the surface, in order to make them explicit and even enhance the environmental quality of urban space.[1]

An example of this approach is the "water square," a new typology for public space that also promotes cultural change, emphasizing the need for people to "live with water." The water square in Benthemplein, Rotterdam (De Urbanisten, 2013) — the first of its

kind to be constructed — channels rainwater into a series of three basins of increasing depth, with the deepest basin only filling after a prolonged downpour. From the shallower basins, water gradually seeps into the groundwater, supporting surrounding vegetation. Rather than being concealed in pipes, the flow is channeled through a series of wells and gutters gushing with water. The heavier the rainfall, the more intense the volume, making apparent the immediacy of the relationship between water and the urban form.

The deepest basin may only be filled a dozen times per year, but it is how the square functions in the absence of water that is especially innovative. The architects asked the surrounding community how they could be supported, and through a participatory process derived a unique, resilient development centered around the neighborhood's

above: A "palace for the people": main hall of Moscow's Komsomolskaya subway station. Photo Alex Segre/Alamy.com/Argusphoto

young people. As the architects described it, "When it's dry, the square is a feast for active youth to sport, play and linger. The first 'undeep' basin is suitable for everybody on wheels and whoever wants to watch them 'doing their thing.' The second 'undeep' basin contains an island with a smooth 'so you think you can dance' floor. The deep (third) basin is a true sports pit suitable for football, volleyball and basketball, and is set up like a grand theater to sit, see and be seen. On each entrance we created more intimate places to sit and linger." The water square delivers on its primary purpose — to protect people and assets from flooding, which is highly disruptive and expensive to recover from. But at the same time, it provides a place for people to connect — both with each other and with the forces of nature.

Human Experience

A desire for visual delight is another human need that the underground can address at the same time as fulfilling its function. A new metro system, for example, does not have to be a uniform sea of beige tiling, responding to the dictates of a least-cost procurement process. If it has a distinctive character, it not only enlivens the daily commute but also helps to reinforce a sense of connection with a place.

This quality of placemaking is something that the Soviet authorities were well aware of when they came to plan Moscow's first subway line in the 1930s. At a time when the West was in the grip of the Great Depression and new subways in cities like New York were of necessity low-ceilinged, utilitarian spaces, Moscow's new stations were conceived as opulent "palaces for the people" where the guiding design principles were a "light" and "bright future" corresponding to the promise of Soviet rule. Highly ornate and individually differentiated, the stations incorporated enormous ceiling mosaics depicting important figures from Russian history, military victories and references to traditional iconography, evoking both an ancient lineage

A NEW FRONTIER

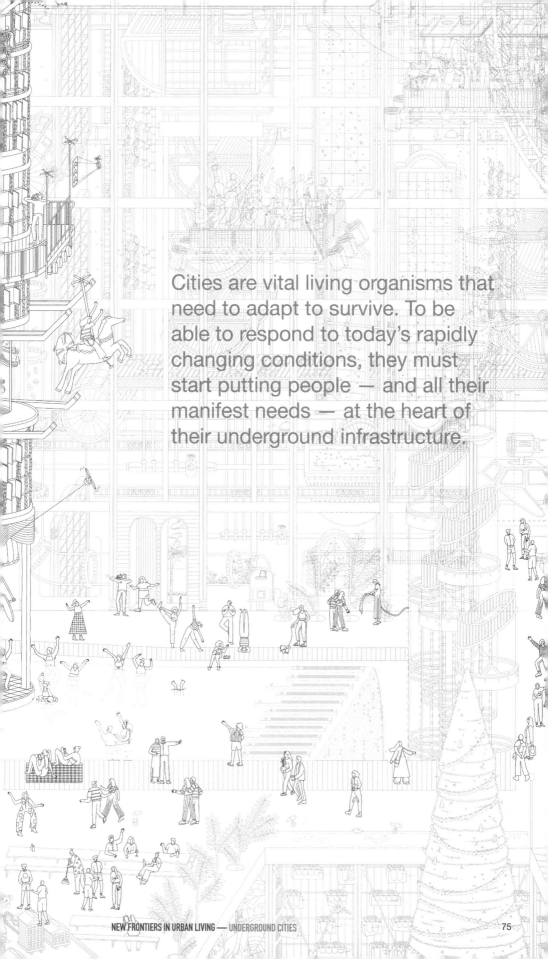

Cities are vital living organisms that need to adapt to survive. To be able to respond to today's rapidly changing conditions, they must start putting people — and all their manifest needs — at the heart of their underground infrastructure.

Stockholm's T-Centralen metro station is painted with motifs from nature. Photo Lingxiao Xie via Getty Images

PEOPLE-CENTERED SPACES

and the new national identity. More than just a means to convey workers to and from their places of employment, the Moscow metro was a powerful propaganda tool, reinforcing a sense of collective identity.

Other cities have been equally adept in using their underground railway systems as canvases for cultural expression. Many of the 100 or so stations that make up the Stockholm metro have individual characters, defined by paintings, sculptures and installations. Here again there is a unifying theme, in the form of references to Swedish history and culture, as in the paintings and mosaics at Stadion celebrating the city's hosting of the 1912 Olympics, the 1km-long painted spruce forest at Solna Centrum, and Bo Samuelsson's screen prints at Telefonplan depicting the area's transformation from an industrial quarter to a cultural district. In Stockholm, art is also combined with nature, as the beautiful bedrock of the subterranean spaces is left exposed to create cavern-like walls of gray or reddish, fine- to medium-grained massive granite or volcanic rock, metamorphosed to form veined gneiss. Together, the natural and the man-made create a distinct sense of place that adds to the multi-layered identity of the Swedish capital.

above: Massive floodwaters descended on Bangkok, Thailand in 2011. Photo Krashkraft Vincent via Getty Images

PEOPLE-CENTERED SPACES

The Underground Movement

On the other side of the world, in the capital of Thailand, we find an example of how people are self-organizing for the benefit of their own communities, finding innovative solutions to the problems they face.

When massive floodwaters descended on Bangkok in November 2011, communities were not provided with accurate and timely information on how to respond. Into this information vacuum stepped an anonymous local group that produced a cartoon video equating the 100 cubic kilometers of floodwater to 50 million blue whales needing to traverse the city to reach the sea. The video, which quickly went viral, described how to help the whales get back to the sea as quickly as possible — making it clear that this would take several weeks — and explained the causes of the flooding, both natural (a heavy monsoon) and man-made (deforestation, urbanization).

Bangkok has subsequently embarked on a major infrastructure development program, installing massive pipes and pumps to help reduce flood risk. It has also invested heavily in providing far more accurate public information about flood hazards and responses. However, no city can afford the program of urban hardening required to protect its citizens from all hazards. As such, these underground movements should be nurtured and celebrated as customized, logical and effective responses to the increasing challenges of surviving and thriving in modern cities.

Using innovative approaches and technologies, we can make new kinds of subterranean spaces that go beyond the purely functional to support myriad aspects of contemporary urban life — making our cities more resilient to climate change, providing spaces of leisure and recreation, while helping communities cohere and co-design their own solutions to life's challenges through new underground movements. In reinventing our underground spaces, we should reflect on and learn from our predecessors' responses, helping our communities to invest for the future while acknowledging its uncertainty and complexity. Cities are vital living organisms that need to adapt to survive. To be able to respond to today's rapidly changing conditions, they must start putting people – and all their manifest needs – at the heart of their underground infrastructure.

HOMO SUBTERRANEUS: INHABITING THE SUBSURFACE

Pamela Johnston

below: Typical layout of Vietnam tunnel complex. Image adapted from T. Mangold and J. Penycate, *The Tunnels of Cù Chi* (New York: Random House, 1985)

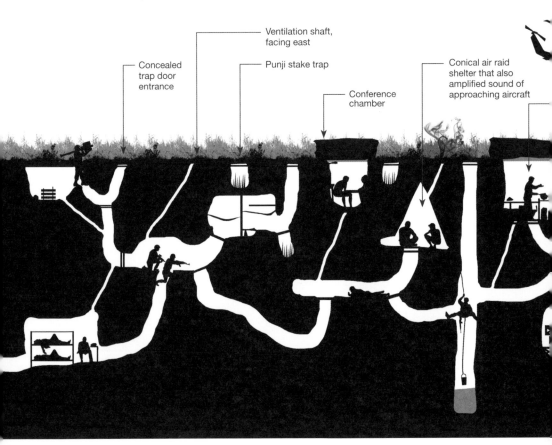

Ventilation shaft, facing east

Concealed trap door entrance

Punji stake trap

Conical air raid shelter that also amplified sound of approaching aircraft

Conference chamber

Remote smoke outlets

en phu" kitchen

Most of us who live in large cities already spend a portion of our days underground — commuting, shopping, eating, going to a basement gym or cinema. But could we imagine extending the use of the underground to make it a regular place of work — even a dwelling place? It's a question that is attracting increasing attention as we explore ways to relieve the pressures caused by climate change and population growth. It's also one that has already been answered in ingenious ways. For millennia, people around the world have made the move underground. Sometimes this is the result of conflict. In Vietnam, nationalist guerrillas fighting first the French and then the Americans developed an extensive network of tunnels that by the mid-1960s stretched for hundreds of kilometers, connecting villages and provinces. In addition to providing for the necessities of life, some tunnels contained field hospitals, weapons factories and arsenals — everything required to wage war.

More often, however, the external threat comes not from other people but from the climate. To escape the merciless heat of the Iranian desert, the inhabitants of old cities in the region of Khuzestan created labyrinthine underground complexes known as "shavadans." Insulated by the earth, naturally ventilated, and cooled by mountain river water, these subterranean spaces would remain at a stable 22C to 25C even when it was 50C on the surface. Each shavadan was focused around a main hall where all the activities of life, both social gatherings and business deals, carried on as usual.[1]

As we contemplate increasingly diverse uses of the underground, there are lessons to be learned from the past, particularly when it comes to reducing our dependence on energy-intensive, mechanical means of cooling and ventilation. Fully integrating the subsurface into the life of the city, however, also requires a shift of mindset. Until now the creation of underground spaces has largely focused on function, rather than the human occupants. To move beyond this utilitarian approach we need to measure the subsurface by the same criteria we use to gauge the quality of a space above ground, recognizing that how we respond to an environment is shaped by a whole host of sensory and psychological impressions related to feelings of protection, comfort and enjoyment. Are we sheltered from the elements? Do we feel secure? Does the space invite us to linger? Is it on a human scale?

Precisely how we perceive underground space — and how we are affected by spending long periods deprived of natural light — are areas where scientific research lags behind advances in technology. Until recently, designers of people-centered underground spaces had to rely on studies, many of them up to 30 years old, that were based solely on observational and self-report methods. Those earlier studies indicate negative attitudes toward working underground, but it is not clear whether these have an intrinsic physiological basis or are rooted instead in social or cultural prejudices — the remnants of thousands of years of religious tradition and human burial practices.

Over the past few years, an extraordinary research effort has begun to address these deficits in our knowledge. Teams from Singapore's Nanyang Technological University (NTU) have embarked on an extensive systematic survey comparing above-ground and underground workspaces in five countries (Singapore, China, Sweden, Norway and the US). Their research examines the interaction of human psychology and health with underground spaces in a holistic way, bringing together specialists in neuroscience, medicine, civil and environmental engineering, business and cultural science. The following sections of the text draw extensively on the literature reviews and preliminary findings of a number of NTU research papers which are in the public domain.[2] After considering the physiological effects of subtracting natural light from the environment, and introducing some new lighting technologies that could increase our sense of comfort in an enclosed space, the text will look more broadly at ways we can counter negative attitudes and change people's perceptions of the underground.

The Importance of Light

Most living things on this planet — not just humans, but animals, plants, fungi and even cyanobacteria — have a natural hardwired body clock that regulates the ebb and flow of their energy over a roughly 24-hour period. In humans, these circadian rhythms are influenced by hormones, meal times and levels of activity, but most of all by light, which is necessarily filtered by the environment, whether it is indoors or outdoors, above or below ground. Alongside rods and cones, the eye has a third photoreceptor system, discovered only in 2002 — a circadian pacemaker that is exquisitely sensitive to ocular light exposure, even in some people who are otherwise totally blind.[3] Exposure to light — and especially to the blue wavelengths of computers and smartphones — suppresses the production of melatonin, a hormone that not only helps us to sleep but also has a part to play in modulating immune responses, blood pressure and enzymes. However, the NTU research suggests that short periods of exposure to daylight in the first part of the day — in the morning, or during a lunch break — can be enough to regulate melatonin levels.

Levels of the hormone associated with stress — cortisol — vary in response to both the body clock and increasing workload, generally being highest in the morning and reducing over the course of the day, with momentary spikes related to work demands. One study found that underground workers have lower cortisol levels in the afternoon than their counterparts above ground, though it did not establish whether this was again caused by dimmer lighting levels, or had more to do with the environment being more stable — or less stimulating.[4]

A large body of evidence confirms the importance of light for health and well-being.[5] For some time, light therapy has proven effective in treating a range of conditions, including depression and sleep and eating disorders. These applications are now being extended beyond the clinical setting. Onboard the International Space Station, for example, fluorescent lightbulbs have been replaced with solid-state LEDs with adjustable intensity and color. The new lighting system, developed by a team led by George C. Brainard at Thomas Jefferson University in Philadelphia, Pennsylvania, is designed to improve the health and cognitive performance of the crew, whose body clocks are subjected to the severe stress of "slam-shifting" as they hurtle around the Earth every 90 minutes, seeing the sun rise and set each time.

More commercially, a new generation of LED lighting is addressing the fact that humans, as a species, are not naturally suited to the standard nine to five working day. Instead our energy and alertness levels generally follow a six-hour cycle, peaking around midday but slumping soon after to reach a 3pm low before the cycle begins all over again, reaching its second peak of the day around 6pm. A

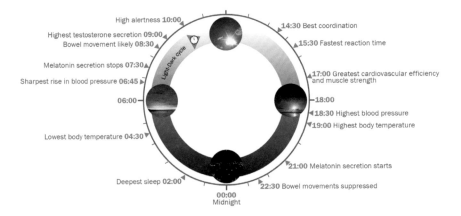

number of manufacturers are marketing "dynamic circadian lighting" with light recipes that you can vary throughout the day. One company promises "faster cognitive processing," "better mood," "better concentration" — the lightbulb as a wonder drug.[6] Research has yet to catch up with the marketing claims. What has been established, however, is that higher intensities of light in the workplace result in higher levels of performance and more positive subjective reports — up to a certain point.[7] After around 650 lux, diminishing returns set in, with increases in fatigue at lighting levels above 1,000 lux. Equally, our eyes become strained when they try to resolve small details in low luminance (below 600 lux) or flickering fluorescent light.

Making an artificial light source more "natural," however, does not necessarily result in an improvement in work performance. A Swedish study found that long-term memory recall was actually reduced when an underground workspace was lit with a cool white light as opposed to the warm white light usually associated with artificial lighting.[8] The researchers concluded that their subjects, confined to a small room, felt overstimulated by a combination of the "natural" light and a lack of privacy.

Spending extended periods in an enclosed environment also reduces our direct exposure to sunlight, the main way our body produces the Vitamin D it requires. A century ago, the most common symptom of Vitamin D deficiency was a softening or mis-shaping of the bones, in the form of now thankfully rarer diseases like rickets. In recent years, researchers have linked low levels of Vitamin D to insulin resistance and type 2 diabetes. Getting enough Vitamin D is not a problem exclusive to the underground — UV-B radiation is also blocked by ordinary window glass — but for underground workspaces, the most obvious solutions are to modify shift patterns and locate rest areas and canteens above ground.

Finding our Bearings Below Ground

After light, a sense of connection to the outside world features high on the list of things that people say they would miss most if they were living or working underground. Confined to a windowless office, workers will often try to compensate for the lack of visual stimulation by supplying their own elements of nature in the form of pictures or indoor plants. A series of studies have demonstrated that the presence of living plants can improve mood and increase attention span while reducing stress. The condition of the plants is generally seen as a barometer for the health of the space as a whole, so a solitary neglected ficus, its last few leaves tinged a desiccated brown, has no known performance-enhancing effect.

A team at Hong Kong Polytechnic University has recently taken this research further, with an experiment investigating not just the impact of indoor plants in underground spaces but also the potential use of artificial windows to increase feelings of comfort and connection with nature.[9] Artificial windows — essentially large display panels with customizable views — are already used in some therapeutic settings: on the ceilings above MRI scanners, for instance, to reduce stress during imaging. For their display panel, the Hong Kong researchers chose a familiar view of a city park. Their underground laboratory, 2.2m by 3.3m, was set up as a generic "living room" — white walls, white curtains, white table, white chair — supplemented, for the purposes of the experiment, with house plants and a large artificial window. The response of the participants — 66 students from the department of engineering, most of them under the age of 25 and around two-thirds of them male — was measured with a response-time task, a room assessment questionnaire and biometrics (EDA – electrodermal activity).

The results confirmed the positive impact of plants on both the perception of the space and the performance of the task. The artificial window, however, while generally seen to reduce the visual monotony of the space, did not appear to contribute in the same way to improving concentration. This preliminary research also made it clear that if a substitute for nature is perceived to be "artificial," then its effectiveness is greatly reduced. Significantly, the female subjects appeared to be more finely attuned to the artificiality of an environment than the male subjects. While the sample base was small, this observation of a gendered difference in the perception of a space confirms findings of earlier studies and suggests an area worthy of further investigation.

How comfortable we feel underground is often directly related to the ease with which we can move through the space. But movement below ground, with its limited points of access and interconnection, is necessarily more restricted than on the surface. In addition, the lack of windows deprives us of the distinctive visual markers that help us to find our bearings above ground. Here, the NTU research points to another gendered difference: men tend to be more sensitive to a perceived sense of confinement in an underground space.[10]

Installing lightwells and skylights — or light pipes, in deeper underground structures[11] — can create a sense of visual and physical connectivity with the surface. Likewise, good signage, higher ceilings and wider corridors can help us navigate through the space. For those spending longer periods underground, having a sense of control over their immediate environment becomes increasingly important. Giving individuals the means to regulate the temperature or lighting of a space has been shown to improve performance and well-being, and the sense of control is further enhanced if the worker is able to carry out tasks in different ways and at different times of their choosing. For the estimated three percent of the population who suffer from severe claustrophobia, however, being underground may trigger very real physiological symptoms — a feeling of oppressive enclosure, or even suffocation — that cannot automatically be eliminated by good design or by reassurances of safety.

In an effort to dig deeper into human responses to the underground, the NTU research is combining field observation with a lab-based methodology using techniques from cognitive neuroscience, including electroencephalogram (EEG) and functional magnetic resonance imaging (fMRI), which measure neural activity.[12] Emphasizing biological and psycho-cognitive aspects rather than traditional psychological explanations, it is exploring a whole battery of effects of our interaction with the underground — on attention, memory, decision-making and impulsiveness, stress, social behavior, emotional and psycho-motor responses, job performance, sleep and other issues related to circadian rhythms. The experimental space allows the team to vary environmental parameters — such as temperature, lighting, virtual windows, air quality — and measure responses both subjectively and objectively, using metrics such as brain responses and physiological responses (i.e. heart rate), among others.

Virtual reality (VR) environments allow for the testing of situations that are too difficult or dangerous to observe in the real world, providing a rich set of data to study. All responses and behaviors can be recorded in an integrated way and the whole sequence of events can be video recorded and played back from any angle. Recent developments in eye-tracking in VR allow for the automatic analysis of visual interest across all the participants in a room.

Eye-tracking, reflecting infra-red light off the surface of the eye, is a widely used method to assess mental effort (via eye blinks and pupil dilation) and visual attention (via gaze direction). This technique

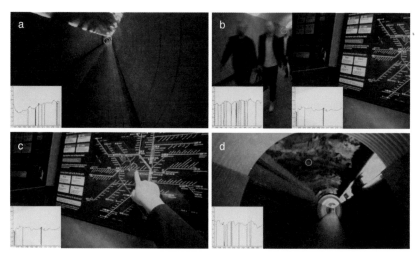

above: Eye-tracking recordings. The red circle indicates where the eyes look, whereas the graph at bottom left indicates eye-dilation, a measurement of arousal. (a) An empty tunnel: the individual looks at the end of the tunnel and the eye dilation is increasing (b) The individual is attracted by the faces and eye dilation is higher compared to the empty tunnel (c) Using eye-tracking we can understand how individuals navigate and use maps (d) Attention attracted to the rock ceiling. Courtesy of Decision, Environmental and Organizational Neuroscience lab (deonlabblog.com), Nanyang Technological University

> " We're made for the light of a cave, and for twilight. Twilight is the time we see best. When we dim the light down, and the pupil opens, feeling comes out of the eye like touch. Then you really can feel color, and experience it. "

James Turrell
American artist

suggests that the addition of plants modifies the perception of a basic underground environment. Rather than the eye seeking out and remaining focused on the means of exit, visual attention is more evenly distributed across the space. But eye-tracking also reveals how our perception is shaped by our surroundings. In a complex urban environment, city-dwellers are less likely to look at other people's faces and more inclined to focus on other salient (preferably inanimate) features — a habit that can cause some distress to incomers from more rural areas until they learn to adapt and turn away their gaze.[13] The same space, too, is perceived differently depending on whether it is empty or crowded — and depending on our mood, there are "good crowds" (for example, the convivial throng of a concert hall) and "bad crowds" (the crush of the rush-hour metro).

Looking to the Future

To date, most research on the use of underground space has focused on compensating for its perceived shortcomings — the relative lack of natural light, the sense of confinement or enclosure. Yet these qualities, in the right setting, also have positive associations. Bright, even light may contribute to the smooth functioning of a space, but dim light and shadow — natural properties of the subterranean — feed our imagination and focus our mind.

Young poets in the bardic schools of ancient Ireland would compose their verse in a completely darkened cell, furnished only with a narrow bed.[14] Marcel Proust famously continued this tradition as he labored for over a decade on his masterpiece, In Search of Lost Time. His workplace was his bedroom, where the walls were cork-lined to dampen sound and the blue satin curtains were tightly drawn to shut out light. A single green-shaded lamp provided just enough illumination to write by.

PEOPLE-CENTERED SPACES

Darkness has a disinhibitory quality. Experienced individually, it can enhance creativity. Experienced in the company of others, in a setting where we feel secure, it promotes sociability and heightens our sensory awareness. We become more attuned to the different qualities of sound, to smells, to our own movement through space, to the presence of others.

The American artist James Turrell has talked of how we are not made for the kind of light that can be turned on at the flick of a switch, flooding a space with an evenly distributed brightness. Rather, he says "We're made for the light of a cave and for twilight. Twilight is the time we see best. When we dim the light down, and the pupil opens, feeling comes out of the eye like touch. Then you really can feel color and experience it."[15]

While it seems evident that there can be no single standardized set of human responses to the underground, the new generation of research should provide us with insights that will help to create underground spaces that fulfill functional needs and are made for pleasure. In this context, it would be interesting to extend the focus of the research beyond the workplace. Rather than a substitute for the space on the surface, the underground could be conceived as a place that generates its own distinct atmospheres, with its own material aesthetics and qualities of light, defined by their fluid relationship with darkness. This would be an underground that is open to a more riotous incursion of nature, an underground that embraces very different kinds of spaces, an underground that allows for all kinds of human activities — a place that makes us feel safe, that provides us with opportunities to stand and linger or sit down and watch the ballet of urban life unfold; a place to talk and listen to others, an arena to exercise and play. In short, a beautiful space, inhabited by people who are there by choice and not simply because they need to work.

BRINGING THE ELEMENTS OF NATURE UNDERGROUND

Lee Barker-Field, AECOM

Until now, the defining characteristic of man-made subterranean space has been its exclusion of nature. Mechanically regulated, hermetically sealed, this most artificial of environments has remained largely impervious to the passing of the seasons, the fluxing qualities of light over the course of the day, the flow of fresh air, the developing forms of living vegetation.

Yet all that is set to change. Drawing on buildings and projects from around the world, the following chapter illustrates some of the recent advances in technology that are opening the underground to the elements of nature and in the process vastly expanding the possibilities for its use. Far from being purely utilitarian, these projects extend the habitable realm of the city. They create social spaces where people can come together and provide shelter in harsh climates; they even suggest a revolutionary alternative to the intensive farming methods that are a major contributor to climate change. Key to these developments is the infiltration of light into spaces deep below the surface of the Earth.

Light
The vitality of natural light can now be captured, in part at least, by artificial lighting systems that change color to replicate the visible cycles and qualities found in the natural environment. In lighting design, we make a distinction between sunlight, which is highly directional, and skylight, which is highly diffuse, scattered in the atmosphere, blocked by clouds or reflected off other objects. Weather conditions affect both sunlight and skylight, but even on a

very overcast day the sky is not totally uniform. The area around the sun's position will be brighter than the rest, and light passing through the zenithal area will be a different color, or spectral composition, becoming brighter at the horizon. These diverse factors give rise to wide seasonal and daily variations. Light levels on a clear sunny day, for example, are around 1,000 times brighter than on an overcast day and 100 million times brighter than on a starlit night.

" Architects continue to deploy daylight in multiple ways and for diverse purposes: to inculcate a relationship between inside and outside; foster a sense of connection to place and landscape; cajole movement through space; attract people to areas of luminosity and shadow; direct attention toward particular colors, textures and features; communicate sacred and symbolic meaning; convey a sense of time passing; enhance or investigate the qualities of materials; foreground the vitality of light and the world; or generate potent interior atmospheres. "

Tim Edensor
From Light to Dark: Daylight, Illumination and Gloom
(University of Minnesota Press, 2017)

right: Global annual temperature map.
Image Lee Barker-Field/AECOM

Temp in Celsius

-5.35   28.25

For underground spaces, these artificial lighting systems can be combined with natural light that is either brought in directly, through openings with optimized geometries and materials, or reflected through specialist light-channeling devices. In New York City, the Lowline envisioned by Dan Barasch and James Ramsey (p. 116) uses satellite technology — solar-tracking optical devices and a solar canopy — to stimulate plant growth in a completely enclosed space. An old trolley terminal beneath the city streets will become the world's first underground urban park.

French architect Dominique Perrault's project for an intermodal transit center in Gangnam, Seoul (p.104) is anchored around another innovative system, the "Lightbeam," in essence an inverted U-shaped structure made of faceted glass and steel panels that reflect and diffuse natural light, drawing it deep underground. Here, the quality of light in the interior varies over the course of the day, responding to the changing colors of the sky. At night, the flow of light is reversed, with "moonlight pipes" casting light from the subterranean interior onto the open space of the park above.

In turn, the extension of the ARoS Aarhus art museum in Denmark by James Turrell with Schmidt Hammer Lassen (p.98) explores the

possibilities of manipulating light to create spaces that are infinitely flexible, with a constantly changing character. The work makes evident the powerful psychological effect of the spectral composition of light, showing that how we perceive colors is highly subjective, shaped by individual experiences and emotions.

By contrast, Junya Ishigami's House and Restaurant in Yamaguchi, Japan (p.112) uses the dilute lighting of a subterranean, cave-like space to conjure a potent interior atmosphere — a world of shadows, mystery and depth, where every room is defined by the variable play of darkness and light.

Air Temperature

Some of the world's most densely populated countries — among them Bahrain, Bangladesh and Singapore — are in the hottest regions, where underground development offers a means of sustainably moderating space temperature. Analyzing decades of satellite data, NASA scientists have found a marked increase in the amount of ultraviolet radiation reaching the Earth's surface over the past 30 years, as human activities have depleted the levels of ozone in the atmosphere. About half of the solar radiation received by the earth is absorbed at the surface. Generally, the ground temperature shows seasonal fluctuations to depths of about 10m to 15m, where the temperature is roughly equal to the mean annual air temperature. Below this, however, the ground temperature remains stable throughout the year. The further down you go, the warmer it becomes, increasing on average 2.6C every 100m due to heat flowing from the interior of the earth. The ground temperature, then, can be higher than the outside air temperature in winter, but lower in summer, and these variances can be harnessed in underground space design to regulate ambient air temperature and humidity levels.

Along with increasing levels of solar radiation, designers of today's cities must consider the urban heat island effect, which means that the city center can be significantly warmer (around 5C) than surrounding rural areas, particularly on nights when the air is still. The effect is mainly the result of covering the natural terrain with hard surfaces constructed of dense materials that retain much of the heat they absorb during the day. Other contributing factors include waste heat generated by energy usage, the displacement of trees and vegetation, which results in a drop in natural cooling effects, and tall buildings separated by narrow streets, which trap and heat up the air between them.

Vegetation
Serving as the green lungs for increasingly congested cities, vegetation is expanding its domain, blurring traditional boundaries between spaces as it thrives indoors as well as outdoors, in above-ground and below-ground environments.

As the presentation of the interior landscaping of Changi Airport shows (p.122), new lighting technologies allow luxuriant decorative vegetation to colonize and soften a technological space. LED horticultural lighting is also increasingly being used to grow food crops beneath our city streets. Many cities now have small underground farms — London's Growing Underground, in a WW2-era shelter in Clapham, produces salads and micro-leaves, while Paris is pursuing a more adventurous culinary route, with a plan to turn a disused subterranean maze in the 20th arrondissement into a "Flabfarm" for edible insects by 2021. An intriguing UK and China collaborative research project, based at Nottingham University (p.128), proposes to multiply the scale of production exponentially. Focused around the re-use of a vast number of redundant coal mines close to urban centers, it would allow for intensive crop production using renewable energy, a minimal amount of water and no pesticides. The scale of these underground farms would also make them effective carbon scrubbers, removing carbon dioxide from the atmosphere.

This kind of re-purposing of underground space is well aligned with current thinking on circular sustainable city planning. An underground space that has outlived its original use because it has been left behind by advances in technology or changing lifestyles can be brought back into service at a relatively low cost, in terms of embodied energy.

In showing us the underground as an integral layer of the sustainable city — a space that not only leaves more room for nature on the surface but enfolds the elements of nature within itself — the projects presented in this chapter offer a fascinating glimpse into what the architecture of tomorrow may look like.

AROS AARHUS: NEXT LEVEL EXTENSION

Schmidt Hammer Lassen and James Turrell

The Next Level extension is a building that explores the possibilities of manipulating light to create spaces that are infinitely flexible, with a constantly changing character. Visualized here is its central space, James Turrell's *The Dome*. Image courtesy of Schmidt Hammer Lassen Architects

An exploration of the space-making capacity of light lies at the core of James Turrell's expansion project for the ARoS Aarhus art museum in Denmark. The American artist has often talked of the "thingness" of light as something you shape with your perception, something that you can touch and hold:

" You don't form it like clay, you don't carve it away like wood or stone. It's more like sound, so you make an instrument that produces it the way you want … That's why I have many spaces you go into, you don't see for 10 minutes. Without focus, without image, without object, what are you left with? You can be left with actually seeing your seeing, how you go about creating this reality that you live with. Often the eyes will create form when it's not there. "[1]

The Next Level extension is the second artist-led addition to the museum, following the Danish-Icelandic artist Olafur Eliasson's *Your rainbow panorama* (2011), which hovers like a luminous halo above the museum's roof, linking it visually to the Aarhus skyline. The new project extends the museum horizontally, in contrast to the existing vertical movement, working with the natural flow of the city to create a public route through the building that forms a bridge between two of Aarhus's cultural nodes — the river and the square containing its music hall.

Developed with the museum's original designers, Schmidt Hammer Lassen, and its director, Erlend Høyersten, the extension provides 1,200m² of subterranean gallery space culminating in a huge semi-subterranean art installation, *The Dome*, 40m in diameter. While the dome rises 9m above the current ground level, the remaining underground galleries are almost completely concealed. Only a change in the surface of the landscape hints at the expansive spaces hidden below.

At the height of the dome, a 6m oculus opens to the sky, bringing light into the space. The color of the clean concrete walls changes in response to the color of the sky, giving the sensation of blending colors inside the dome. Turrell has talked of how the mixing of colors in light requires a relearning of the spectrum, as you can no longer rely on the color wheel. In painting classes, if you mix blue and yellow you get green; if you do the same with light all you get is white light, so you need to have a whole different way of thinking.

For Turrell, the interest lies in the relation between reality and perception. "We think that things are fixed, that we receive the phenomena of the world and are not a part of creating what we behold … We think the sky is blue. We forget to realize that actually we award it its color." For architecture more generally, the project suggests a future direction where the power of perception can be coupled with the manipulation of light to create spaces that are infinitely flexible, their character changing, chameleon-like, in response to changing needs.

Architect/Landscape Architect
Schmidt Hammer Lassen Architects

Artist collaboration
James Turrell

Completion
2020

Client
Aarhus Municipality
ARoS Aarhus Art Museum

Client consultant
Kuben Management A/S

Engineer and subconsultant
COWI A/S

Contractor
Per Aarsleff A/S

Visualizations
Beauty and The Bit

THE LIGHTWALK, GANGNAM INTERNATIONAL TRANSIT CENTER (GITC)

Dominique Perrault Architecture

The "marker" of the GITC reveals the scale of the site. © Dominique Perrault Architecture/ Adagp

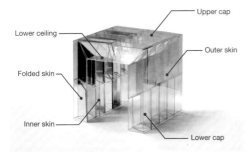

Labels on diagram: Upper cap, Lower ceiling, Outer skin, Folded skin, Inner skin, Lower cap

above: Schematic diagram of Lightbeam system.
© Dominique Perrault Architecture/Adagp

Central to architect Dominique Perrault's conception of "groundscape" is the idea of a marker that reveals the scale of the site. For Gangnam International Transit Center (GITC), a subterranean multi-modal transit hub and commercial center, that reference measurement is supplied by the Lightwalk, a 10m-wide glass structure that spans two major road arteries and orients movement around the airport-sized piece of infrastructure. Like a ruler, the Lightwalk extends in a single straight line through the entire 550m length of the site. In its mid-section, it forms the core of a new urban park — a "Green Land" framed on all sides by trees. The planting creates a foreground that allows a transition between the intimate human scale at ground level and the surrounding city scale of high-rises and wide streets. At a larger scale still, the Lightwalk is conceived as a monumental Land art intervention in the spirit of works by the American artist Richard Long. Through minimal means, it sets up a dialogue with the wider landscape — with the Han River and the distant mountains.

The Lightwalk is also the facade of the transit center, forming not only a membrane between the external environment and the interior space but also an optical instrument dedicated to bringing light where it is most needed. The quality of this light is constantly in flux. During the day, "sunlight pipes" capture and concentrate light and bring it down into the interior. At night, the flow of light is reversed, and the same pipes cast "moonlight" onto the park, giving it a special atmosphere.

References
Each underground space, including the train platforms and vehicle drop-off areas, is visually connected to the central axis and the

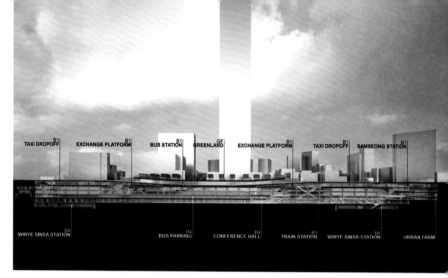

TAXI DROPOFF | EXCHANGE PLATFORM | BUS STATION | GREENLAND | EXCHANGE PLATFORM | TAXI DROPOFF | SAMSEONG STATION

WIRYE SINSA STATION | BUS PARKING | CONFERENCE HALL | TRAIN STATION | WIRYE SINSA STATION | URBAN FARM

above: Perspectival section, GITC, Gangnam, 2017–23.
© Dominique Perrault Architecture/Adagp

grand hall, with its 30m-high ceiling. The scale of the space and the presence of natural light create the feeling of being in an outdoor train station — even for passengers entering at basement level four. In this respect, the Lightwalk draws on the familiar nineteenth-century typology of the grand metropolitan train station. In its linearity, it also echoes the covered arcades of Paris or the Galleria Vittorio Emanuele II in Milan. As in those arcades, a glass roof shelters the pedestrian space below from the elements while accommodating the ebb and flow of natural light and the everyday life of the street.

The structure that guides light down into the interior, the Lightbeam, refers to the French Pampille or Tassel system, traditionally used to increase the brightness of candle chandeliers. Adding to these properties, the Lightbeam is also used as a technical instrument for controlling temperature and humidity.

Bringing Light Underground
Structurally, the Gangnam International Transit Center (GITC) shell is conceived as two linear buildings facing each other. The Lightbeam is an independent entity inserted into the gap between them and surrounded by a clear and freely accessible safety space of 1.5m on either side.

The optics of the Lightbeam system can be broken down into three main functions, whereby the top horizontal part filters the incoming daylight, the lateral vertical parts reflect and transmit the light, and the lower caps at the very bottom disperse the light laterally. The fully glazed curtain wall facade is designed to favor, as much as possible, the entry and diffusion of natural light. Once it has been filtered, every ray of light is used.

Axonometric section, GITC, Gangnam, 2017–23.
© Rayus/Dominique Perrault Architecture/Adagp

Though its subtle game of reflections and transparencies appears complex to the visitor's eye, the Lightbeam is in fact a very simple object. It consists of an inverted U-shaped steel and glass structure, the Cortex, at the center of which are large suspended mirrors. The horizontal part of the U-shaped glass is composed of the "upper cap," which is the outdoor plane, and its indoor equivalent, the "lower ceiling." In between the two is the folded skin of faceted glass and steel panels which reflect and diffuse the natural light.

Each side of the Cortex is composed of two parallel transparent bonded glass panels, an outer and an inner skin — a glass plane facing the inside of the GITC, and a multi-angled glass prism facing the center of the Lightbeam, which refracts the natural light into a color spectrum.

The bottommost part of the Lightbeam, the lower cap, is again formed by alternating opaque perforated metal panels and transparent prismatic glass panels that refract the natural light as it is channeled through the vertical sides, ensuring it is uniformly diffused through the interior. As the light is diffused, it is also broken down into the colors of the rainbow.

" Public underground infrastructure for urban transportation are just like skyscrapers: They are punctual spikes of density in the urban fabric," writes Dominque Perrault. The GITC, with its Lightbeam, is a project that fully exploits the potential of the interface between the deep ground and the dense city, in keeping with Perrault's dictum, "The groundscape is to cities what the mycelium is to fungi: an underground root system that allows cities to grow without deforming their grounds, without losing their continuity. "

The multiple reflections and refractions of natural light bouncing between the panels and the steel frame make the light vibrate. The light that is diverted to the lateral vertical parts of the Lightbeam is reflected downward — to this end, around half the panels in the vertical elements and the folded skin are reflecting, so the incoming light bounces from panel to panel and propagates toward the center of the building. Mirror-polished steel mullions amplify the effect. Both sides of the U-shaped glass volume then serve as light cannons, transmitting natural light vertically through the Lightbeam. In selected areas, where the floor lighting requires it, transparent panels in the outer skin remove some of the rays and direct them to where they are needed.

above: Placing the transit center underground has allowed for the creation of a new urban park. Day view of the "Green Land."
© Dominique Perrault Architecture/Luxigon/Adagp

Within a system of more than 10,000 elements, the repetition of identical modules allows for the large-scale reproduction of standardized components, facilitating the construction process and maintenance but also making it a flexible object, easy to adapt to future change. The composition of each panel is carefully chosen from a range of materials in response to lighting, ventilation or structural needs: fully transparent, colored, printed, photovoltaic or electrochromic glazing alternates with mirrored, polished and blasted metallic surfaces to create a kaleidoscopic optical effect. This multifaceted reflective texture allows the Lightbeam to draw strength from its environment; first reflecting and fragmenting the surrounding landscape and the colors of the sky and then constructing them anew.

Lighting the Lightbeam

The ceiling lighting in the interior hall can be supplemented by LED spotlights fixed to the lower cap of the Lightbeam and the reflective gutter that runs alongside it. The upper cap is lit by horizontal LED bar spotlights in stainless steel enclosures with light-diffusing surfaces. The lateral faces are lit by orientable spotlights in tubular stainless-steel enclosures. At nighttime, from the outside, the Lightbeam appears as a river of light running through the middle of the park.

A Comfortable and Performative Facade

By reducing lighting energy consumption, the Lightbeam increases the efficiency and sustainability of the infrastructure. Indeed, lighting simulations indicate that a 10m-wide Lightbeam enables 90 percent of the Forum space to be naturally lit with an illuminance above 300 lux, which is the lighting comfort standard in Korea.

The Lightbeam also plays a central role in the building's overall performance, directing and redistributing natural light where it is required. The correct specification of low-iron glass maximizes the transmission of daylight and has a positive effect on the indoor climate, allowing for interior gardens. A combination of opaque and transparent panels, high-performance coatings and enhancers with reflective surfaces ensures solar protection and increases thermal comfort.

The Lightbeam's central position within the GITC makes it possible to have natural ventilation throughout the building, in the form of operable air vents. In case of emergency, these vents become a natural smoke exhaust system. Additional operable air vents and thermal pipes running across the Lightbeam's steel frames regulate its temperature. In this way, it serves as a heat reservoir in winter and as protection from the hot and humid exterior in summer.

above: Night view of the "Green Land" park: at night the flow of light is reversed and "moonlight pipes" bring light from the GITC up to the surface.
© Dominique Perrault Architecture/Luxigon/Adagp

Design leader
Dominique Perrault Architecture (DPA/Paris)

Consortium
DPA, Paris
Junglim, Seoul
Space Group, Seoul
Yooshin Engineering, Seoul
Sunjin Engineering, Seoul
Teso Engineering, Seoul

Expertise
Topotek 1, landscape architect, Berlin
Jean-Paul Lamoureux, acoustic adviser, Paris

Client
Seoul Metropolitan Government

Location
Yeongdong-daero Street, Gangnam, Seoul

Competition: July–October 2017
Completion: 2023

Site area: 60,000m²
Built area: 167,000m²

Program:
· Multimodal hub: 95,000m²
  New train station (four new lines: GTX A/C, KTX, Wirye-Sinsa) 46,850m²; extension of the existing metro stations, Samseung (Line 2) and Bongeunsa (Line 9) 16,305m²; bus station 3,180m²
· Park: 32,000m²
· Commercial complex: 72,142m² (event hall, exhibition spaces, cafes, restaurants, art galleries, offices)

HOUSE AND RESTAURANT, YAMAGUCHI

Junya Ishigami + Associates

The cave-like spaces of the house and restaurant allow the feeling of being at one with nature. Photo Satoru Emoto @ SARUTO

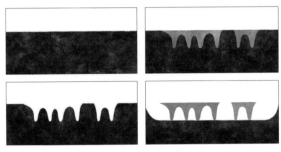

above: Construction sequence clockwise from the top left: a series of holes were made in the ground and concrete poured into them, then the earth around the concrete was removed. Image Junya Ishigami + Associates

For this house and restaurant located in Yamaguchi in the south of Japan, the client, a chef, said he wanted the atmosphere of an old space, as he felt it offered a calmer, more comfortable setting for dining. But how does one create an old atmosphere in a new building without having to wait for the passage of time and the patina that comes with use? The answer, here, was to make a cave-like space that provides the feeling of being within nature, allowing us to believe that the restaurant might always have been part of this environment.

The first step of the construction was to excavate narrow passages, 3m deep, out of the ground. Digging the earth, removing the rock or soil, is the archetypal way of creating a subterranean structure, only in this case the digging was not to carve out the final space but to make the molds for the concrete structure. The pour was done in a single day — over a period of around seven hours — to ensure the consistency of the material. Once the concrete had set, the areas in between were excavated to find the spaces that lay within the field of soil, in much the same way that an archaeologist digs down and uncovers the rooms of an ancient dwelling, one by one.

Each room within the building has a distinct atmosphere, with different qualities of light and shade depending on its relation to the internal courtyards. Those courtyards also serve to separate the house from the restaurant. The poured concrete columns were originally going to be cleaned, but as they emerged from the soil they had a character reminiscent of Japanese earthen construction — a timeless form of architecture — so it was decided to finish them in the same way.

Designed to resemble natural rock, the result is a cave-like space that blurs our usual reference points between natural and man-made, interior and exterior, above and below ground.

below: Construction views: the concrete pour was done in a single day. Photos Satoru Emoto @ SARUTO

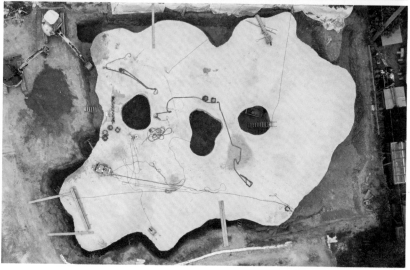

THE LOWLINE, NEW YORK CITY

In the space-challenged heart of a city, the idea of allocating land for a park often meets stiff competition from rival needs such as housing and revenue-generating commercial developments.

In New York City (NYC) in 2009, less than four miles from where the Western hemisphere's tallest skyscraper was steadily rising towards its eventual symbolic height of 1,776ft, designers were developing a contrasting vision for maximizing land use. As One World Trade Center reached for the skies, they explored the potential of the city's depths, applying a fresh perspective on the future of the built environment with the creation of the world's first underground park. At 60,000ft^2, the new park is the size of a football field.

Inspired by the city's Highline project, the Lowline seeks to repurpose a run-down part of NYC's transit system. Twenty-five feet below Delancey Street is the disused Williamsburg Bridge trolley terminal. While the site has lain abandoned since the service was discontinued in 1948, the highway above has grown into one of NYC's busiest thoroughfares in one of its most densely populated, rapidly gentrifying, and least green neighborhoods — three related yet diverse and critical challenges that many cities today can identify with. The Lowline co-founders, Dan Barasch and James Ramsey, visualized the creation of a year-round green space for city dwellers. Turning convention upside down, they located their urban oasis below ground.

To bring this vision to life, they needed innovative technology to channel sunlight into the subterranean space, license to use the site from the city government, and community engagement in the idea. As the project was intended to be for the public good, it made sense that the public should be invited to participate in its creation. License was subject, among other considerations, to proof of concept, and that was reliant on funding. Aptly, James Ramsey is a former NASA satellite engineer, turned architectural designer for Raad Studio, and Dan Barasch's career includes strategy and marketing for Google. Pivotal to the concept's uniqueness and robustness is the ability to transfuse natural sunlight into underground spaces. The daylight technology of the South Korean company, SunPortal, was selected for integration into the conceptual design. A system of remote skylights and fiber-optic cables will capture sunlight from nearby rooftops and channel it onto the reflective surface of a distributor dish that will diffuse the natural light around the space. Concentrated through this technique, the light is 30 times the intensity of unadulterated sunlight, more than enough to allow photosynthesis and the propagation of the underground vegetation and to negate the need for electric lighting during periods of sunshine.

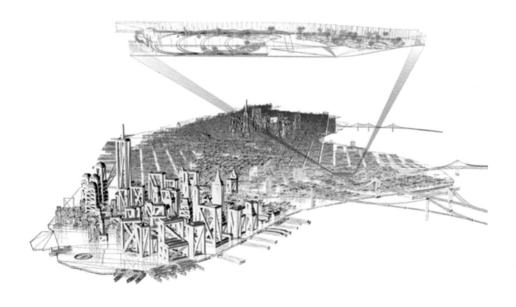

In 2012 a Kickstarter campaign for a prototype Lowline Lab raised US$155,000 from 3,300 donors globally, the greatest number of supporters for an urban design project the platform had ever experienced. The funds enabled the experimental version of the Lowline to be set up in a nearby warehouse that was as dark and abandoned as the site of the eventual park. The lab opened in October 2015 and attracted more than 100,000 visitors in its 15 months of operation. In July 2016 the city government gave the green light to realize the project, although without any public funding commitment.

As critical as proof of concept for the daylight technology was engaging with the people who live in the neighborhood to give them a hint of the experience that the future park could provide. The landscaped environment and a series of organized activities set about dispelling the fears that are often associated with underground space, such as confinement, ventilation and encounters with vermin, most notably rats. The lab reached out especially to the city's youth, inviting them to participate in imagining the infrastructure of the park. Such engagement is bringing people together as a community, helping to build the area's social infrastructure for the future.

The Lowline's power to capture our imagination is many-fold. It is now legendary that a tree frog found its way to the pop-up park and flourished. If a park can be created beneath one of the most crowded areas of one of the world's busiest cities, with all that humans love about parks — natural light, flora and fauna — how many more hidden and abandoned underground spaces beneath our space-starved cities can we reinvigorate and reintegrate in a similar way? As cities cover more of our planet, and as a growing number of the world's population live closer together without feeling close to each other, the Lowline provides a replicable solution to achieve a harmonious balance of green, hard and social infrastructure.

Founders
Dan Barasch and James Ramsey

Proposed location
One-acre former Williamsburg Bridge Trolley Terminal, below Delancey Street, Lower East Side of Manhattan, New York

CHANGI AIRPORT, SINGAPORE

John Endicott, AECOM

Luxuriantly rampant vegetation has become a feature of Singapore's cityscape. Where the highways of northern Europe might have center dividers of concrete, the city-state has a profusion of crepe myrtle, cat's claw ivy, trumpet trees, oleanders and bougainvillea. This fusion of the urban and the natural extends even indoors, to the highly technological environment of the airport, where each of the four terminals has around 1,500m² of soft landscaping, with planting and some temporary displays. The guiding philosophy is "if you can touch it, it's alive."

To minimize the risk of importing pests or diseases, the airport operates its own nursery, bringing on flowering plants for temporary displays as well as propagating trees and foliage and ground cover for permanent planting. Plants are prepared for display indoors by progressively reducing the intensity of light at the nursery for two to three weeks beforehand.

Because of the large covered areas, the permanent plants depend almost entirely on artificial light. Different light frequencies have been trialed, but most areas are lit at about 4,000 lux, which is less than normal daylight and primarily intended for human comfort. The lights

go off at night (23:00 to 07:00).[1] Reducing the intensity and the duration of the light saves electricity and, crucially, slows the growth of the plants, making them easier to maintain.

The selection of plants is based on experience, with a bias toward forest plants that have adapted to living under the shade from a higher canopy. Three species of ficus have proved particularly successful, both for their aesthetic qualities and because they have less active roots, which are less likely to block drains.

The plants are rooted in a manufactured growing medium with a large proportion of clean sand and a very small organic content. The mixture varies according to the type of plant and its location: fertilizers are applied as pellets. Irrigation is through pipes at ground level, using NEWater (high-grade reclaimed water); wastewater is returned to a water treatment plant.

While the choice of slow-growing plants reduces the need for pruning, a major maintenance task is removing the fine dust that accumulates on the leaves. Although plants are sprayed with a fine mist three to four times a day, this is not completely effective and leaves still have to be cleaned manually.

In addition to the areas of permanent planting, there are large displays of movable plants. A feature of Terminal 3 is the 300m-long green wall with racks holding a mixture of plants. The green wall has a considerable textured depth, with some plants having grown to one meter. The lighting is enhanced at the top and the types of planting vary according to the intensity of the light, brightest at the top and darkest at the bottom.

The airport authority's 12 years of experience in cultivating plants helped to prepare the ground for

the new Jewel lifestyle destination at Changi. Designed by Safdie Architects, the 10-story complex — five stories above ground, five below ground — is focused around an indoor Forest Valley, a terraced garden with 2,300 trees. Jewel's distinctive torus-shaped facade, made of tessellated glass and steel, has at its apex an oculus that showers water down into the center of the landscape environment cascading another two floors below ground. More than 200 species of plants are fed by the mists of this "Rain Vortex," which is itself fed by Singapore's frequent and powerful rainfall. Natural rainwater is recirculated and flows at a rate of more than 10,000 gallons per minute, providing cooling and airflow and collecting significant amounts of rainwater for re-use in the building.

Hugely ambitious, the project is conceived not just as a facility for air travelers but as an extension of Singapore's public realm, available to everyone in the city. There are walking paths through the terraced gardens, as well as an adventure park with bounce nets and mazes. Surrounding the gardens is a five-story retail marketplace that also includes a 130-room capsule hotel and an iMax theater. Five stories underground, below the glass mall, is a food court with 280 vendors and, hidden from view, baggage handling systems and IT infrastructure.

A focus on long-term planning played a major part in the realization of Jewel. The city-state's Urban Redevelopment Authority (URA) gives architects clear briefs that go far beyond the spatial, volumetric zoning guidelines of most conventional building projects, addressing objectives such as climate adaptation and integration with existing public transport networks. Any project submitted to the city's Building Construction Authority has to include 3D models made with the BIM software, Revit, which makes it easier to analyze the building in various ways. Incentives are also given for using prefabricated parts and incorporating sustainable features. What Jewel shows us is a city made more livable by the dialogue between a creative designer and forward-looking urban planning groups.

Manager
Changi Airport Group

Head of Horticulture, Changi
Khaja Nazimuddeen

UNDERGROUND FARMING

Emma Lowry, University of Nottingham

Future farming: indoor system combining fish aquaculture with hydroponics, cultivating plants in water under LED lighting.
Photo josefkubes/Shutterstock.com

Underground farms have already taken root in many cities around the world. Specializing in low-bulk, high-value produce like micro-leaves for salads or delicate strawberries, they have shown that growing food underground is not just good for the environment — consuming less energy than conventional agricultural methods — but also commercially viable. Now researchers at Nottingham University in the UK are proposing a dramatic increase in scale, exploring technologies that would allow intensive crop production in existing, but obsolete, networks of coal mining and civil air defense tunnels. Located beneath or close to city centers, this new kind of subterranean farm could help to feed rising urban populations while also forming a sink to absorb carbon dioxide.

For the next two to three years, the research will focus on the potential to develop the concept in the UK and China. Professor Saffa Riffat, project lead and chair in sustainable energy at the University of Nottingham's Faculty of Engineering, explains that in the UK alone there are more than 1,500 redundant coal mines, while China has over 12,000 abandoned mines (0.6 million cubic meters), 7.2 billion cubic meters of tunnels and about one billion cubic meters of civil air defense tunnels. Professor Riffat is working with research fellow Professor Yijun Yuan, a specialist in sustainable energy and mining engineering.

A variety of crops could be grown in the subterranean farms using hydroponic planters, with plant roots fed with nutrient-rich water. Groundwater could be used directly, or water could be condensed from ambient air — coal mines in particular are often humid spaces. Colored LED units (run on renewable energy or off-peak power) would enable photosynthesis in the absence of sunlight. The subterranean environment remains a stable temperature and is largely unaffected by the seasons or extremes of climate, so crops could be produced year-round, even in arid regions. A further advantage of this approach is its potential to improve food safety. In many countries cultivated land and water are heavily polluted. About one-fifth of arable land in China, for example, is contaminated with levels of toxins greater than government standards (2014 data), and 14 percent of domestic grain contains heavy metals such as lead, arsenic and cadmium (2015).

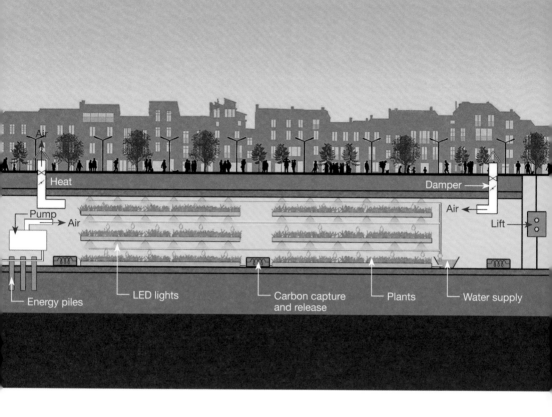

Carbon dioxide (CO_2) is required for plant photosynthesis. As subterranean spaces are well suited to carbon storage, the farms would use carbon capture and release systems, which would also reduce CO_2 concentration in the atmosphere. The researchers envision using advanced control systems, including sensors and remote controls, to monitor crop production. Harvesting would be fully automated.

The subterranean farms represent an alternative to vertical farming systems, a relatively recent adaptation of the traditional greenhouse. While vertical farms are suitable for use in cities, producing high crop yields on a small land area, the tall glass structures are expensive to manufacture and install, and require a large amount of water and energy for heating and cooling. They are also vulnerable to extreme weather conditions.

For Professor Riffat, however, the argument for underground farming is not just based on the ideal conditions it provides for plants to thrive in a closed environment with less oxygen and enriched levels of CO_2. It comes down to a question of making the best use of precious land resources: "In terms of the rationality of the biological chain and the biological space," he says, "crops are best located underground, leaving the ground surface for human and animal activities."

MOVING PEOPLE, TRANSPORTING GOODS

Technological advances are redefining our understanding of time and distance. Against this backdrop, two visionary projects are being developed in anticipation of future lifestyle needs and aspirations. One is an underground regional logistics network in Switzerland, the other involves land travel at flight speed. As the pneumatic science that underpins Hyperloop travel illustrates, however, we cannot always predict which way technology will swerve or how society will evolve. Planning necessitates an inbuilt flexibility so that it can respond to our ever-changing needs.

OF LOOPS, PUMPS, PIPES AND HYPE

Carlos López Galviz, Lancaster University

To many in the early part of the twenty-first century, pressurized capsules, vacuum tubes and a new generation of motors and air compressors are the solution to traffic congestion — a means to transport goods and people at high speed between Los Angeles and San Francisco, or between Helsinki and Stockholm, Dubai and Abu Dhabi, Edinburgh and London. But this is not the first time that compressed air and pneumatic tubes have been the future of transit. George Medhurst patented a pneumatic tube system for conveying people and parcels in England in 1810: laid "upon or underground," his invention was designed to propel packets of letters "with the velocity of 100mph"; Baron von Rathlen's compressed-air vehicle is reported to have reached a more modest 12mph in 1848; John Gorrie's US patent from 1851 provided the basis for the use of compressed air in refrigeration, key to the transport of food and other perishables a few decades later.

In other spheres, the history of pneumatic technology stretches much further back. Compressed air and hydraulic pumps were prominent in the intricate and often extraordinary mechanisms found in the subterranean chambers in ancient Egyptian temples; Ctesibius of Alexandria constructed a wind-gun making use of compressed air around 120 BCE.

Later applications included Papin's experiments in the 1670s with "an air pump driven by a water wheel" — which, significantly, was to enable transmitting motive power at a distance — and the pneumatic pumping engines installed in the mines of Chemnitz by Hoell in 1755. Early piston pressure machines of this kind were soon followed by a range of equipment for the construction industries, both structural and ornamental, as well as specialist tools ranging from medical instruments to artist's tools and cleaning devices in homes.[1] This wide array of uses gained both momentum and focus during the nineteenth century, particularly in cities. What we can learn from this process, and what a contrast between it and current developments such as Hyperloop might reveal, are two of the questions I explore in this brief piece.

From around the 1860s on, pneumatic tubes would help to alleviate street congestion by taking some of the traffic generated by letters and parcels off the streets in cities like London, Paris, Berlin, Boston, Chicago, New York, Prague and Vienna. Through a system that connected post offices and their branches to railway stations, banks, government offices, hotels, department stores and other businesses, mail was first sorted and subsequently pumped through pneumatic tubes to destinations across the city. In large cities, the system supplemented the telegraph as well as the post's own

cadre of cyclists and runners, helping to reduce the pressure that the concentration, breath and intensity of communication placed on existing infrastructure.

The London Dispatch Company was among the first to provide this service, opening a line a few months after the first section of the Metropolitan Railway, the world's first underground railway, started operating in January 1863. The tubes covered 2.75 miles, between the Eversholt branch of the General Post Office (GPO) near Euston Station, the terminal of the London and North Western Railway, and the GPO's headquarters in St. Martin's Le Grand in the City of London. Mail traveled in cars propelled at speeds that could reach up to 60mph, covering the distance from end to end in nine minutes. On occasion, the operators did the journey themselves, inside the cars, shot through the tube, with one description praising "the air being fresh and cool." Creating a sufficiently air-tight environment to secure the vacuum needed for the system to work proved challenging. Leaks were common. After just over 10 years, the company went bankrupt and the service — along with the infrastructure that supported it — was forgotten for at least 20 years.

In Paris the experience of the pneumatic post, and compressed air more generally, was different. The "pneu" and other pneumatic networks used the sewers, which meant that the initial costs were significantly lower. From a test line laid in 1868 to connect the Bourse (Stock Exchange) with one of the main telegraph offices in Grenelle (across the Seine), the pneu developed into an extensive network of pipes — around 550 miles at its early 1960s peak — that allowed Parisians to send anything from theater tickets to bill payments to covert messages about political machinations from one end of the city to the other within the space of two hours. Embedded within the postal services — and culture — of the French capital, it remained operational until 1984, by which time it had long been overtaken by the telephone and telex.[2]

The use of pneumatic tubes and compressed air in postal services was the result of a twin process or, more accurately, a process with twin forces, namely a) the spatialization of different functions, that is, the fact that a network would support a particular kind of service and need (post, transport, water, electricity, and so on) and b) the specialization of these services and needs (first-class letters, express trains circumventing the city center, gas cookers in houses powered and heated by electricity, among others).

Networks develop to accommodate functions that are then spatialized and specialized. Often, they do so as layers, sections (a railway viaduct, a motorway, a walkway, a sewer) that cross one another, partly to avoid bottlenecks, partly to separate the matter, the things and the beings that are "on the move." Undergrounds, characteristically, are the spaces that accommodate the very functions that sustain the city above (sewers, catacombs, shelters, cellars and storage rooms, metros, seed vaults and more).

To an important degree, the emergence of networks of pneumatic tubes for postal services was an urban creation. Maintaining communication flows between people and institutions was a challenge where that communication was dense, frequent and urgent — a situation characteristic of cities. To be sure, not all cities embraced the idea, or had the need of accommodating communication in pneumatic tubes. There were also significant differences between a capital city and regional centers, notably ports. By 1910 the British Post Office Telegraphs company had over 34 miles of tubes in London transmitting more than 32,000 messages a day across 41 offices and branches (including "spares"); in the port of Liverpool, a network of around 5.6 miles carried 10,000 messages a day across nine offices, while the industrial powerhouse of Manchester merited only five branches and around 1.2 miles of pipes, through which 3,000 messages were transmitted daily.[3]

A different kind of challenge is posed when the flow of communication is not just within a city, but between two or more cities — between Paris and London, for example. In 1885 Jean-Baptiste Berlier proposed to link the French and British capitals with a pneumatic tube for the transport of first-class letters. It would be more than a century before his idea of a fixed connection was realized in the form of the Channel Tunnel, which opened in 1994. Letters and parcels are, of course, only one of the many traffic flows the tunnel accommodates, alongside high-speed passenger trains, goods trains and motor vehicles.

And so the space that a network or a line serves and creates is important, as is the level of specification that the network supports. Early twenty-first-century developments on the transport of goods and people are part of the same trend. Hyperloop is set to solve traffic congestion between cities, not within them. It is closer to the

below: Map showing the Paris compressed air network in 1962, when it extended over 550 miles. Black denotes the old network, red the new. Image SUDAC

Channel Tunnel than it is to pneumatic post — in some respects, it is a hybrid, resembling mainline railways, though running on compressed air rather than steam, diesel or electricity. The first such "atmospheric railway" line opened in 1843. Taking passengers from Kingstown to Dalkey in southeast Dublin — a distance of one and three-quarter miles — its vacuum was provided by a 100hp single-cylinder steam engine. While its speed was limited by the need to brake at bends in the line, it could reach speeds of more than 40mph. A retrospective account commented that the line "worked for many months with regularity and safety throughout all the vicissitudes of temperature which occurred."[4] Whether the reporter truly understood the vicissitudes of the Irish weather is something

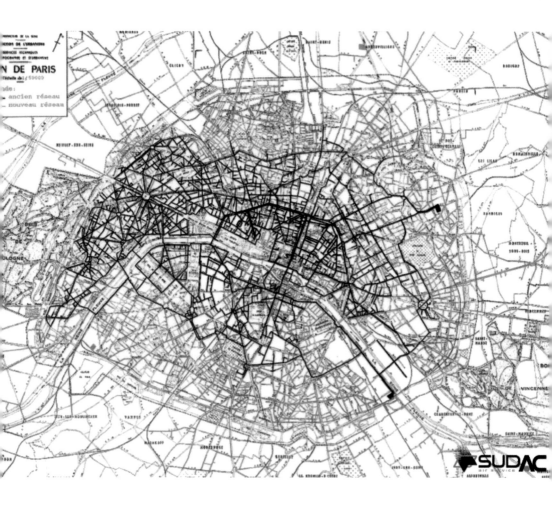

we will never know. After just over 10 years, the line was closed and converted to a broad-gauge track integrated with the rest of the Irish railway network.

As critics, commentators and supporters of the Hyperloop alike have observed, the concept of pressurized capsules traveling in vacuum tubes powered by a combination of motors and air compressors isn't new. What is new is the interest and momentum it has gathered, in large part triggered by a successful PR and fundraising campaign. Elon Musk's Hyperloop Pod competition has so far issued and attracted entries for four calls in January 2017, August 2017, July 2018 and July 2019. The only criteria by which entries are judged are "maximum speed with successful deceleration (i.e. without crashing), and all pods must be self-propelled." Engineering student teams from the technical universities of Delft and Munich and the Massachusetts Institute of Technology have taken most of the accolades so far.

Hardt Hyperloop, the Dutch spin-off winners of the first 2017 Pod competition, are working toward the first European Hyperloop route. Its website asks us to "imagine a world where distance does not matter," where a solar-powered, emission-free "network of cross-border cities, all connected in one network" can take us from Amsterdam to Paris, say, in 38 minutes. Among their partners the website lists the Dutch railways, DHL, Danfoss, Strukton, Tata Steel and of course Delft University of Technology itself. In turn, Hyperloop One, founded in 2014 by Josh Siegel and Shervin Pishevar, has all the ingredients of the start-up story — a whiteboard in a garage in Los Angeles, an innovation campus in LA's art district, a test site in the desert near North Las Vegas. Building on the momentum and global reach of the calls — which extend as far as India and Saudi Arabia — a number of feasibility studies are currently underway, including in Colorado, where Hyperloop and the Department of Transportation entered a public–private partnership, supported by AECOM.[5] Virgin Group became a partner in October 2017; Richard Branson was named chairman by the end of that year.

If Hyperloop is the Answer,
What is the Question?
To many at the turn of the
twentieth century, compressed
air was the "modern Atlas" of
industrial civilization, the titan
that would carry the weight of
progress in the century ahead.

Inside the Devloop, Hyperloop One's Nevada test track.
Photo Hyperloop One

above: Tintoretto, Studies of a Statuette of
Atlas, 1549 © J. Paul Getty Museum

To many at the turn of the twentieth century, compressed air was
the "modern Atlas" of industrial civilization, the titan that would
carry the weight of progress in the century ahead (Dikeç and López
Galviz, 2016). As we know, that role was taken first by electricity
and then by nuclear power. The analogy between Greek mythology
and contemporary developments in technology, however, is useful
in another respect. Atlas was condemned to stand at the ends of
the Earth, holding the heavens aloft for all eternity, in retribution for
rebelling against Zeus. Jacopo Tintoretto's rendering of Atlas, one
of many produced by Italian artists in the sixteenth and seventeenth
centuries, captures most eloquently the effect this punishment had
on the body of the titan, namely, how much of his own anatomy was
transformed by carrying the weight of the celestial sphere.[6] The fact
that it does not show the sphere makes it all the more compelling: the
titan's anatomy is shaped by that which he carries, whether it is there
or not. It is a body shaped by what is absent.

Extending this metaphor, we could replace the celestial sphere with
the heavenly promises of future transportation and ask, what would
be the effect of imposing the Hyperloop on the body of Los Angeles,
San Francisco, London or Edinburgh? Should its promise — both
what it highlights and what it leaves unsaid — shape any one city?
And, if so, at what cost?

The growth of cities, the mobility of goods and people, and the
emergence and development of networks are all interdependent. As
the population of a city grows, new networks are needed: roads and
ways for transport; waterpipes connected to reservoirs and treatment
plants for both potable and wastewater; lines of communication first
through the post, the telegraph, the telephone and, more recently,
the internet; conduits for energy and motive power for houses and
businesses, for running a range of appliances as well as keeping
them cool or heated. At the same time, the size of cities expands

and contracts according to the networks of which they form a part, regionally, but also nationally and globally. Undergrounds have been a central part of — and have played a decisive role in — this dynamic for centuries, in some cases millennia. As things stand in the early part of the twenty-first century, far from receding, their role is becoming ever more essential for cities to function.

Whether Hyperloop will prove its worth and develop as a collection of lines or as a network connecting cities has yet to be seen. A recent exhibition at the Victoria and Albert Museum in London, "The Future Starts Here," asked its visitors "If Mars is the answer, what is the question?" The Eddington Transport Study (2006) raised the very same question in relation to HS2, the new high-speed railway line in the UK, which is due to reinforce connections between London and the West Midlands, increasing capacity, frequency and, of course, speed. The need that Hyperloop is set to meet and the spaces that it will generate and connect are still in the making. At the same time, the infrastructure it requires is not the kind that might be redeployed for a different use. What solution Hyperloop provides is contingent and entirely dependent on trends that we know will change over time. Will people continue to travel between San Francisco and Los Angeles in 20 or 50 years? Will inter-city mobility increase in the future? Will citizens have a say in the process of envisioning what their everyday patterns of travel or behavior might be in 2040 or 2070? We know well where the sights of Musk and Branson are set: toward space. Are we all prepared to become modern Atlases? If Hyperloop is their vision, what is ours?

Further Reading
M. Dikeçc and C. López Galviz, "The Modern Atlas: Compressed air and cities c.1850-1930," Journal of Historical Geography 53 (2016), 11–27. P Dobraszczyk, C. López Galviz and B. L. Garrett (eds.), Global Undergrounds. Exploring Cities Within (London and Chicago: Reaktion Books, 2016).

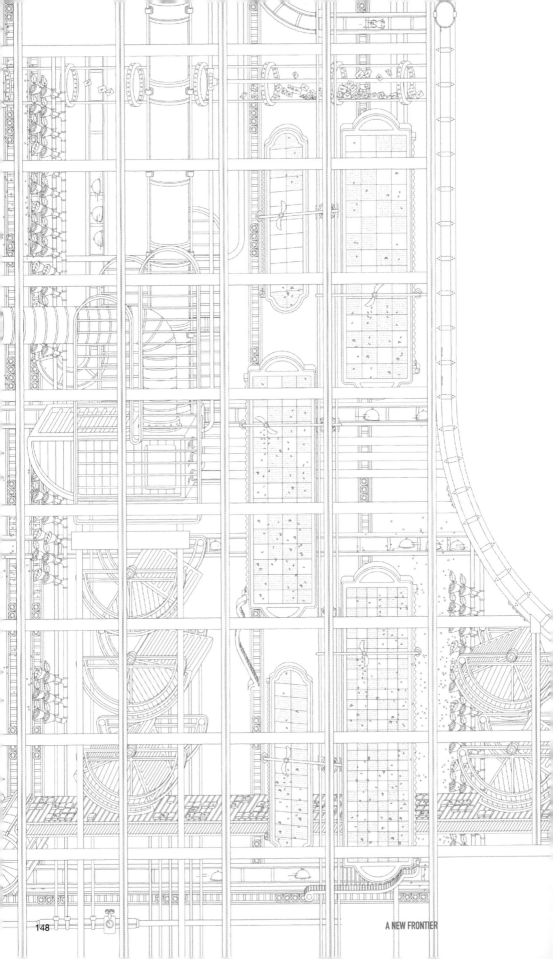

A NEW FRONTIER

UNDERGROUND LOGISTICS

Cargo Sous Terrain

One hundred billion. It's one of those ungraspable numbers, a measure on the same scale as the grains of sand in the desert or stars in a vast swathe of the cosmos. But it's also the volume of parcels that will be shipped globally in 2020, according to the Pitney Bowes Parcel Shipping Index. The figure grows year on year, in line with the inexorable rise of e-commerce. For the sake of comparison, the 2016 total was 63.6 billion.

It is becoming increasingly urgent to find a more sustainable means of handling this goods traffic, with its heavy burden of road congestion and pollution.

One proposed solution is to return to an old form of transport, the airship, which was once the most advanced and luxurious means of air travel, but which stalled after disasters like the crash of the Hindenburg in 1937. A new generation of airships is being born, made with new technologies and new materials, and filled with helium rather than explosive hydrogen. Today's designers share a vision of convoys of airships plowing through the skies at a rather sedate 220kph, carrying payloads of up to 500 metric tons. The new craft can take off and land with the precision of a helicopter and — crucially — require no supporting infrastructure between the two ends of connection, allowing them to access many regions not currently served by road or rail. Cost is the obvious drawback, with each airship having a price tag of around €40 million.

A more agile (and somewhat cheaper) airborne alternative would be the use of drones, although current models have a small payload — generally around 20kg — and a limited range. Their operation also tends to be affected by windy conditions. Added to the question of legislative restrictions on their use, there is the matter of societal resistance from people unhappy at the prospect of the air swarming with drones.

A third solution turns not toward the skies, but digs deep into the earth, with an ambitious plan for a comprehensive underground logistics system powered entirely by renewable energy. Cargo Sous Terrain (CST) envisions a 500km network of tunnels that would link production centers and distribution hubs across the north of Switzerland, cutting heavy goods traffic on the roads by up to 40 percent. Above ground, electric vehicles and bicycles would ensure the "last-mile" delivery of goods from the city hub.

Access to the CST system is provided via the hubs, which allow for fully automated loading and unloading. Vertical lifts feed the goods into the tunnel network: by this stage they are already bundled, so their subsequent micro-distribution is prepared in advance. Transport below ground, through a three-track tunnel, operates on a similar principle to an automatic conveyor system, with driverless vehicles picking up and depositing pallets or modified containers from the lifts and ramps. The vehicles run along electromagnetic induction rails, operating around the clock at a constant speed of about 30kph. Smaller packages are carried along a rapid overhead track attached to the roof of the tunnel.

The project seems to be backed by the necessary political will. The Swiss Federal Council has opened a period of consultation on the required new legislation, and the building permit and planning phase will start with the passing of the CST law, expected in late 2020. The city logistics and the IT infrastructure for the system are already being developed in advance of the tunnel construction work. The first 70km section of the CST network, which will connect Switzerland's largest city, Zurich, with its main logistics hub, Härkingen-Niederbipp, is planned for completion by 2030.

Binding assurances of investments of 100 billion Swiss francs (circa US$10.5 billion) have been made for the first phase of the project, up to construction permit approval. The total cost of building the first section, including software, 10 hubs and vehicles (both underground and above ground), is an estimated 3 billion Swiss francs. A further 30 billion will be needed to complete the rest of the network, which by 2050 will run between Geneva and St. Gallen, with additional branches from Basel to Lucerne and from Bern to Thun, and will serve more than 80 distribution hubs.

Which brings us to the question of who will pay for this vast infrastructure project. The perhaps surprising answer is that CST is a private-sector initiative, led by a consortium that brings together diverse interests, among them Swiss supermarket chains, banks, Zurich airport, the Swiss telecoms and postal services, the energy producer and distributor BKW, the logistics concern Panalpina and the waste disposal and transport company Schwendimann. A large stake is also held by a Chinese investor, reflecting the interest in this development in Asia Pacific, which is the world's largest regional parcels market by value (41 percent). And because construction approval procedures are much faster in China than in Europe, perhaps that is where we will see the first large-scale instantiation of this new concept in logistics.

above: Lift system connecting the surface with tunnels below ground. Image CST

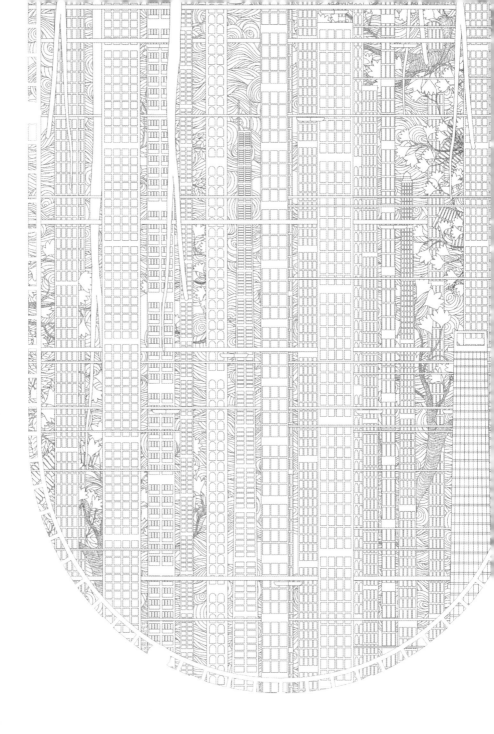

A third solution turns not toward the skies, but digs deep into the earth, with an ambitious plan for a comprehensive underground logistics system powered entirely by renewable energy.

NEW TECHNIQUES OF REPRESENTATION

Faster, smarter, better — the mantra is universal, whether blank-slate planning or working on an existing built environment. The key to better outcomes lies in another form of infrastructure, one that is built, not with bricks and mortar, but with data and artificial intelligence tools based on Building Information Modeling (BIM).

With BIM, a 3D data-enriched model can be expanded to facilitate the assessment of sequencing and scheduling (4D), detailed cost analysis (5D) and even facilities management (6D). Linking these additional "dimensions" provides a clearer view into the health, progress and risks associated with a project throughout its entire lifecycle.

Below-ground projects in Paris and Hong Kong provide a glimpse of two ways technology is enabling new approaches and impacts, using virtual and mixed reality to bring space to life. Even as these new techniques gain momentum, changing the ways we manage and deploy our underground space, what will we be able to achieve in the future, when 5G turbo charges the speed at which data is collected, connected and communicated? Can we build up a holistic picture of previously uncharted territory, enable real-time collaboration across multiple parties, and test the robustness of hitherto untried notions on virtual versus real people?

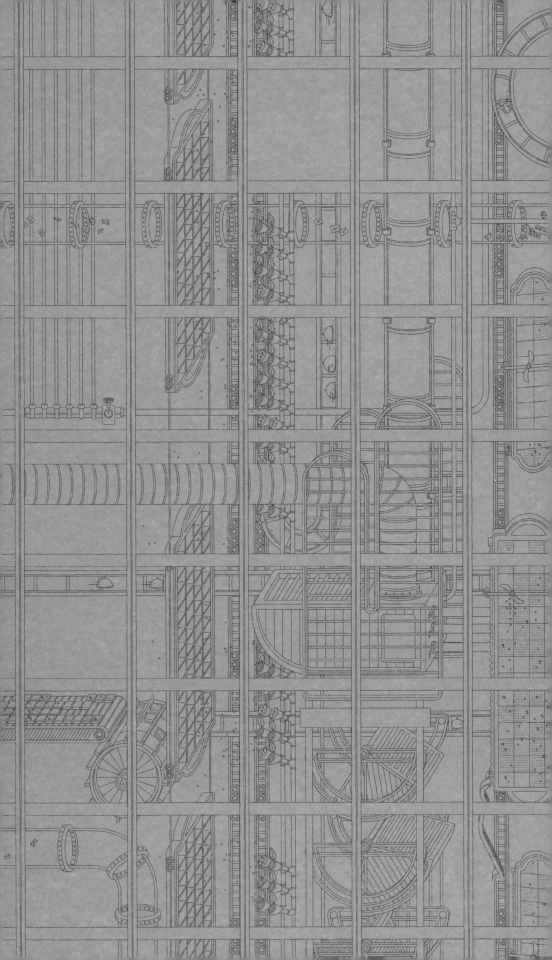

RECLAIMING THE SUBTERRANEAN NO MAN'S LAND OF PARIS LA DEFENSE

Monique Labbé, Jean-Pierre Palisse
and Jean-François David, Ville 10D

The Ville 10D — Ville d'idées (10D City — City of Ideas) National Research Project was set up in 2012 to consider how extending the use of the underground could contribute to a more sustainable form of urban development. Bringing together around 30 researchers from a range of disciplines, it has created analytical tools for approaching key issues of underground urbanism. How can you optimize development to make it attractive, adaptable, safe and resilient? How do you communicate the conditions of the site and the potential impact of the project? How can you create positive interactions — social, economic, environmental — between the surface of the city and its subterranean dimension? Now in its final stage, Ville 10D is refining these methods as it applies its research to real sites, working to establish best practice guidelines.

One such site is the business district of La Défense, built from scratch in the 1960s according to the model of slab urbanism, which placed technical functions and transport flows below the ground in order to free up the surface for human occupation. The multi-level basements, then, were not designed for people but were constructed around road and rail traffic, logistics and parking — an approach that left behind vast, hard-to-access volumes that were never mapped out and remain empty to this day. However, with the impetus provided by the development of the new Grand Paris Express subway line, these residual spaces have become potentially precious land resources.

above: The business district of La Défense was built from
scratch in the 1960s according to the model of slab urbanism.
Photo Alessandra Pezzota/Alamy.com/Argusphoto

The project asks what happens when urban infrastructure needs to
evolve. How do you turn these unused voids into active settings for
urban life, connected with the rest of the city? It highlights obstacles
to change, such as the fragmentation of structures of governance.
And it focuses, in particular, on new means of visualizing such
sites, with the creation of a modeling tool — a 3D model of the
underground — adapted to the development projects envisioned for
La Défense. This is initially a tool for understanding the space and
generating new ideas. Could it also become a means of managing a
complex transdisciplinary project?

The "No Man's Land" of La Défense
Our studies showed that the established instruments of urban design,
based on the continuity of space and the alternation of public and
private realms, are not applicable to the underground levels of La
Défense, where there is a division between public space, which
unfolds horizontally, and private space, which operates vertically. This
division may be less visible than the divide between urban use and
technical use, but it is no less restrictive. Moreover, the theoretical
divide embedded in this urban model — between pedestrians above
and cars below the slab — does not exist in reality. People walk
along underground service ways after they have parked their cars.
Employees leave the towers through the basements after office
hours. And for cyclists, the basements are the only means of access.
What seems obvious is that the human presence is everywhere and
that people have to be reintegrated into every aspect of the design.

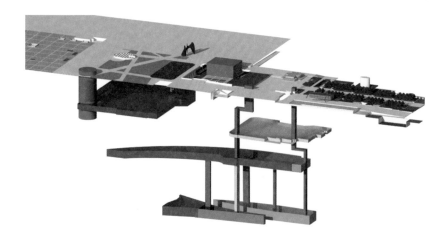

While La Défense is constantly changing on the surface, as new towers rise and old ones are demolished, the underground remains unaltered.[1] Studies of the isolated volumes have been carried out in the past, but none of their recommendations could be implemented, in part because of the fragmented approach to the administration of the spaces. Until recently the governance of La Défense was split between two distinct entities: one responsible for urban planning, the other for the daily management of the district. The creation, in 2018, of a new administrative body fusing these two areas of competence was an essential first step toward establishing an approach that encompasses the site in its entirety, including its erratic, ever-changing human dimension.

The change in governance structures meant that a steering committee could be assembled around the development authority for La Défense, bringing together the various actors involved in transport, services and business, all of whom have a vested interest in the renewal of the district. Learning from the previous deadlock, the new administrator asked Ville 10D to look beyond established rules and practices and introduce new ways of thinking across the board.

Moving Below the Surface
Navigating the underground requires a different approach from movement on the surface, where there are numerous visible markers in the form of buildings or trees, for example. Ville 10D's research into the mechanisms by which we orient ourselves in space highlighted three key issues. First, the brain uses different pathways depending

on the distances involved (near or far), with implications for signage and visual aids to navigation. Second, cognitive strategies vary widely between individuals. Third, to increase the ease of use of the underground, it is crucial to conceive of the space in multiple layers — and thus in three dimensions. Reproducing a fixed layout over several floors allows people to build up a reliable and intuitive understanding of the space and the different ways they can move through it — similar to their experience of moving above ground. By contrast, when there is a radical break in the layout from one underground level to the next it is very difficult to maintain a sense of connection with the surface.

And it is precisely this question of how to break the isolation of the underground — how one enters and exits the cavity — that holds the key to integrating the underground into the spaces of everyday use.

The development authority is progressively introducing "motion" into the locked environment under the slab. Its first step was to install a bar in the most accessible area of La Défense, on the side closest to Paris. After that, a former parking lot, also with a relatively high degree of openness toward the exterior, began a second career as a café, coworking space and exhibition venue. The most ambitious plan, however, is to bring life to an impressive underground volume called the Cathedral, covering 6,400m^2, with 12m-high ceilings. Our study takes this vast space as its center, radiating out from and continually returning to it.

New Modes of Visualization

Ville 10D aims to develop a mode of visualization — a 3D modeling tool — adapted to the development projects envisioned by Paris-La Défense. Such a model already exists for the above-ground structures, but stops at the surface of the slab.

The land surveyor provided a set of longitudinal and cross sections of the perimeter of the cathedral. Further reliable geometric data was obtained from a map of the esplanade of La Défense, with geo-referenced coordinates. Transferring these 2D layouts into a BIM software program allowed us to determine the virtual volume of the project and define the basis for further development of the mapping.

Any project of this scale necessarily involves specialists from many different fields — planners, designers, geotechnical engineers, geologists, among others — each with their own means of modeling the underground space. After making an inventory of these varied modeling formats we are now defining standards that will make it easier to handle and compare the information they contain. To create a degree of consistency, we are compiling a graphic matrix that displays a sequencing of the renders (or 3D visualizations) as 2D compositions. The matrix builds up a full picture of the extent of the Cathedral project and places it within a functional context that includes other areas of La Défense. It will serve as the basis for the collaborative work of the next phase of the project.

The visualization goals relate to the broader recommendations derived from Ville 10D's research, namely to conceive of the underground as a dimension of the urban project; to enhance the multifunctional use of sites and the connections between underground spaces; to reinforce cooperation and consultation and to share tools of knowledge, assessment and projection.

What we are aiming for is a 3D modeling tool that will convey not only the required technical profile but also the spatial configurations and the atmospheres and activities unfolding in the interior, allowing all the players involved in the project to come around the model to share their visions of the future. In the case of La Défense, this approach is being applied to a project that will determine which structures are fixed and which have the capacity to be changed to define new networks, passages and flows. In both the construction of the new train stations and the larger effort to increase the attractiveness of the area, it is the reinvention of the underground that holds the key to the renewal of the high-rise district.

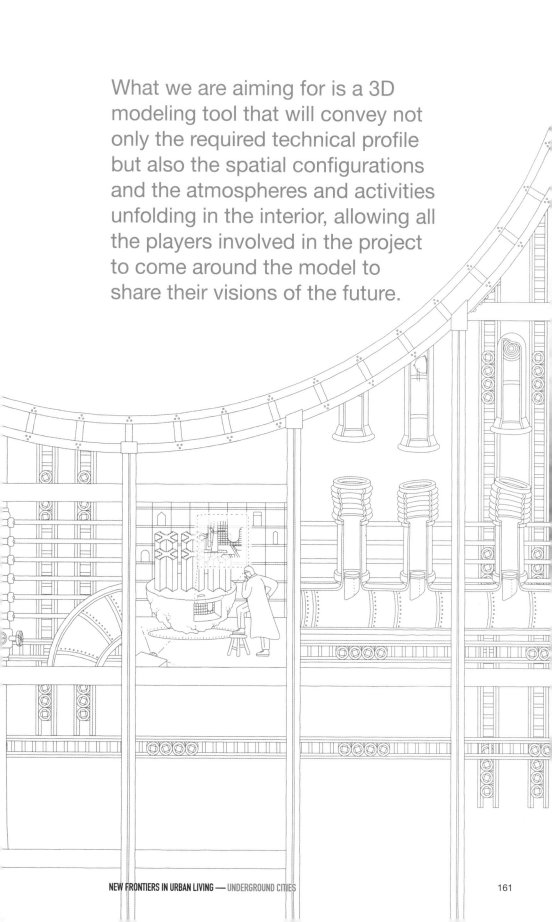

What we are aiming for is a 3D modeling tool that will convey not only the required technical profile but also the spatial configurations and the atmospheres and activities unfolding in the interior, allowing all the players involved in the project to come around the model to share their visions of the future.

INNOVATIVE TECHNOLOGIES FOR PLANNING AND DESIGNING UNDERGROUND SPACE

Thomson Lai and Roger Luo, AECOM
Jeffrey Chun-fai Wong and Tan Tin-lun Yeung,
Civil Engineering and Development Department of the
Hong Kong Special Administrative Region Government

The use of innovative technologies to improve communication among the different parties involved in the planning and design process is fast gaining traction in the architectural, engineering and construction industries. Building on this capacity, AECOM, in collaboration with the Civil Engineering and Development Department (CEDD) of the Hong Kong Special Administrative Region (HKSAR) Government, has explored ways of integrating the latest Virtual Reality (VR) and photogrammetry technologies with more widely used techniques such as Building Information Modeling (BIM) and 3D spatial data. The project presented here is a feasibility study on the planning and design of a conceptual scheme for underground space development.

While Hong Kong has a long history of using the underground for commercial and public facilities, most of these developments are standalone projects with few connections, either lateral or vertical, to the city around them. In dense urban areas, the presence of building substructures, subways, MTR running tunnels, box culverts and other conduits for utilities tends to limit the availability of sites for exploring underground space development opportunities. In this respect, an urban park close to a Mass Transit Railway (MTR) station offers a prime opportunity to create synergy with the existing urban context.

The park is set on hilly terrain surrounded by densely developed multi-story buildings of mixed residential, commercial and retail use. For the initial planning, capturing the existing environment in a 3D model was an important first step, making it possible to study the park and its spatial relationship with a wide range of at-grade facilities. But while there was an abundance of 3D digital data on existing buildings and infrastructure in the public domain — and specifically in the database compiled by the Lands Department of the HKSAR Government — there was insufficient information on the park, as shown by the 3D spatial model of the study area prepared using the available digital data and aerial photographs (overleaf).

To build up a more complete picture, area-specific photographic imagery was used to create a photogrammetry model that enriched the level of detail on the park, in particular the hard and soft landscape elements, and identified specific areas of interest. Integrated with the 3D spatial model, this created a site reality model that allowed the designers to familiarize themselves with the topographic setting, take measurements of the space, and better understand how the project would relate to the existing environment.

In tandem, a BIM model based on the architectural design model was developed for effective communication between the various parties involved in the preliminary stages of the design. The BIM platform provided a virtual environment in which designers, planners, engineers, consultants and client representatives could walk through — and consequently talk through — the different components of the project.

The comprehensive BIM model was then further combined with the site reality model to generate one for visualization that could be hosted on a 3D desktop viewer. The most powerful aspect of this

visualization model is its compatibility with VR technology, which allows the design to be viewed in a 3D manner at 1:1 scale. While the VR simulation has similar functionalities to conventional and desktop-based 3D modeling techniques — e.g. walk-throughs and fly-throughs — it also gives users a heightened sense of reality.

Reviewing the requirements for the VR setup, such as user-friendliness, we identified two levels of visualization. For the first, more straightforward approach, the visualization model was used to produce a set of 360-degree panoramas as the basis for a 1:1 interactive model suitable for a mobile VR device. The low setup cost means that a number of mobile VR devices can be deployed at a single venue, so project information can be effectively shared between different parties. The model can also be used in public consultations, with the selection of the 360-degree panoramas tailored to highlight key aspects such as the integration of the scheme with the existing park environment. Additionally, for wider public outreach, a series of panoramas can be hosted on a project webpage.

For full immersion, which allows for a more detailed design review, the use of a computer-connected VR device is being explored. This would allow users to interact with the virtual underground space design at a real-world scale by using hand controllers for viewing and "experiencing" details of the design components.

above: Site reality model
formed by integration of
photogrammetry reality
model and 3D spatial model.
© AECOM/CEDD

below: 3D spatial model of the
study area. © AECOM/CEDD

The purpose of the two platforms is to present the design in different immersive levels. The images below show representative views on the web-based environment and VR interface.

A further advantage is that the use of the visualization model is not limited to the illustration of design details, as the data can be converted to other software for more detailed analysis, such as shadow, noise and traffic impact assessments. A 4D simulation can also be performed for visualizing the construction process of the underground space with an assumed construction program.

The integration of all the spatial data results in a combined 3D model that can be visualized by all user parties. The figures opposite show sample rendered images from the visualization model.

Until now, the integration of these innovative technologies has seldom been investigated within the framework of a single project. What this study demonstrates are the clear benefits for all parties involved in the planning and design of the conceptual scheme for underground space development in densely populated urban areas. Designers, planners, clients and consultants are able to visualize the components of the design at a 1:1 scale in a way that cannot easily be matched by conventional 2D and 3D desktop software. For the wider public, in turn, the immediacy of the presentation brings the project and its full potential to life.

above: Interactive model on web-based environment (top) and VR interface (bottom). © AECOM/CEDD

above: Sample rendered images of the existing
environment in the study area © AECOM/CEDD

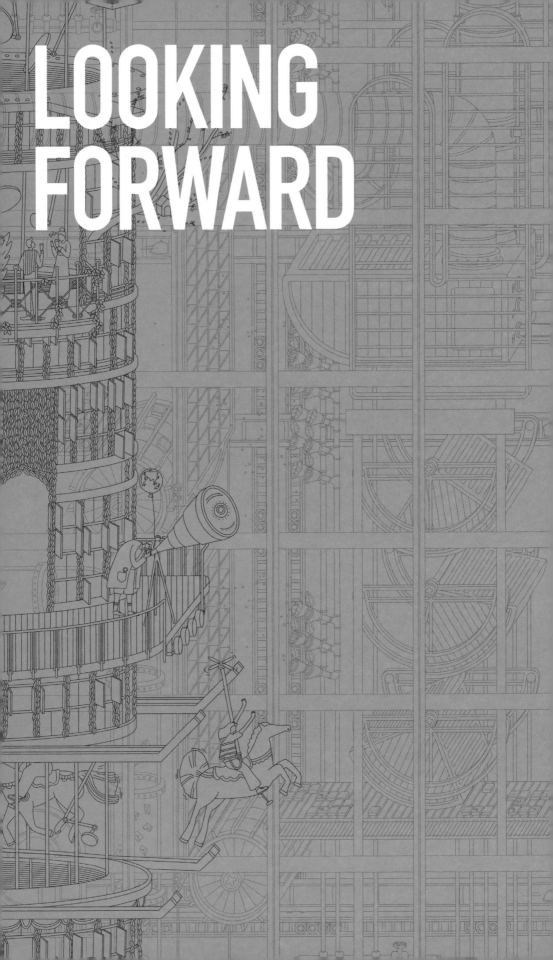

LOOKING FORWARD

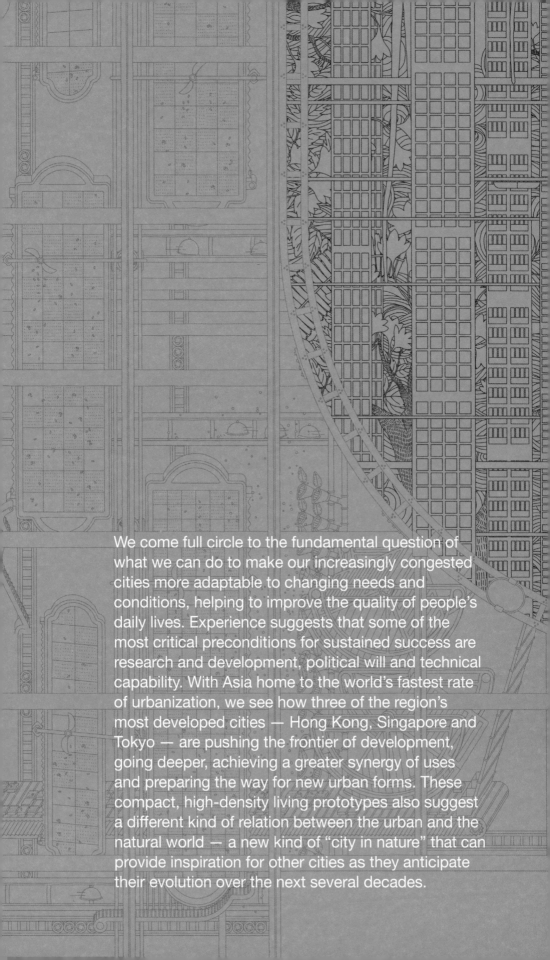

We come full circle to the fundamental question of what we can do to make our increasingly congested cities more adaptable to changing needs and conditions, helping to improve the quality of people's daily lives. Experience suggests that some of the most critical preconditions for sustained success are research and development, political will and technical capability. With Asia home to the world's fastest rate of urbanization, we see how three of the region's most developed cities — Hong Kong, Singapore and Tokyo — are pushing the frontier of development, going deeper, achieving a greater synergy of uses and preparing the way for new urban forms. These compact, high-density living prototypes also suggest a different kind of relation between the urban and the natural world — a new kind of "city in nature" that can provide inspiration for other cities as they anticipate their evolution over the next several decades.

PUSHING THE BOUNDARIES OF UNDERGROUND SPACE

Peter Ho, Centre for Strategic Futures,
Strategy Group, Prime Minister's Office,
Republic of Singapore

For a long time, underground space has suffered from a bad reputation in the popular imagination. In his famous science fiction novel, The Time Machine, H.G. Wells invented the "Morlocks," a primitive species — descended from human beings — that lived underground. Indeed, the prevailing wisdom is that people do not live underground. When they do so, it is always *in extremis*, like the Londoners who sheltered in the Underground during the worst of the Blitz, or the Viet Cong who used the tunnels of Củ Chi as a base of operations during the Vietnam War, or the residents of the opal mining town of Coober Pedy in South Australia who still live underground to escape the blazing desert heat.

It is not surprising that, until recently, underground space was only spasmodically exploited in urban planning, reserved for a few important functional purposes like transport, sewerage or bomb shelters, or developed to avoid the need to obtain agreement with owners of property on the surface. Today, the situation is changing. The rapid pace of urbanization, especially in Asia, is putting a squeeze on the availability of above-ground space in congested cities like Hong Kong, Singapore and Tokyo. As a result, the subterranean environment is increasingly seen as an asset to be exploited in a much more systematic way, with new functions being added to the hitherto limited inventory.

Because of the high costs and complex engineering involved, the development of underground space at scale cannot be undertaken without long-term planning and a clear strategic vision. In this regard, foresight is needed to identify the future demand for underground space and the factors that will shape the urban environment. Foresight is especially important because subterranean developments tend to be long-term projects and permanent in nature. Arguably, foresight must be accompanied by imagination, to break out of the boundaries of conventional thinking, move beyond conservative plans and practices, and instead disrupt with new ideas and game-changing concepts.

The common thread among those who have integrated underground space into the urban environment is the way that their imagination is literally pushing the boundaries of the urban eco-system, accompanied by foresight as a crucial companion. What is now considered commonplace often started as a "wild idea," subject to the scorn and ridicule of the skeptics in its day. For me, two great examples of imagination and foresight, both from some 150 years ago, are the construction of the London Underground and Chicago's development of a sewerage system to radically improve sanitary conditions on the surface. Instead of digging tunnels, Chicago created artificial underground space by jacking up buildings and roads in the city center by about one to two meters, thus raising the level of the city's surface under which the new sewerage system would run. It was a singular act of breakthrough thinking combined with bold engineering. What might be the "wild ideas" of today that could help to make our cities better as land becomes an increasingly scarce commodity?

Although planning and engineering vary — influenced by geology, which impacts engineering options and costs — government plays a key role in the unlocking, deployment and governance of underground space. The hilly terrain of Hong Kong has naturally lent itself to cavern developments for large utility plants, and the city now master plans the development of its cavern systems. Singapore has developed its version of an underground master plan to guide how subterranean space can be developed and used; while Tokyo shows the way in the construction and maintenance of its extensive underground pedestrian networks through partnerships between municipal governments and the private sector. Without the insights and active participation of government, it is hard to assess the direction of factors such as demographics, technology, economic structure and climate change, and how those will shape the needs of our future urban environment.

For Singapore, my home, the 1980s represent the beginning of our underground journey, when we built part of our mass rail system underground. Soon after, in the 1990s, we started to consider building our Underground Ammunition Facility (UAF), the city-state's first cavern development, in solid granite rock in the center of the island. The international safety codes on the underground storage of ammunition then in existence, including the proximity to built-up areas on the surface, were deemed unsuitable for Singapore's unique geology. The scale of the project also presented many engineering challenges that could not be tackled just by acquiring off-the-shelf technologies. The Ministry of Defense embarked on a Technology Development Program to devise new shock codes and technologies in order to minimize land sterilization while achieving a safe and economic design. The resulting cavern freed up about 300ha of surface land, amounting to 90 percent land savings compared to above-ground storage. New explosives storage standards were also developed and subsequently incorporated into NATO's safety manuals.

In anticipation of a future in which climate change causes extreme storms that the current drainage infrastructure cannot cope with, we are now looking at how to collect excess stormwater through an island-wide network of tunnels feeding into an underground reservoir cavern. These projects — experiments on a large scale — showed the strategic potential of underground space in land-scarce Singapore. So, the government decided that the underground space should be developed systematically. This is now being realized through the establishment of an underground master plan. In tandem, the government has created the legal framework for ownership of underground space, supported by the creation of a geological database and compilation of the first comprehensive database of underground infrastructure and utility services in Singapore.

However, experimentation should not be limited to government. To boost the spirit of innovation and encourage private-sector involvement, governments can and should facilitate industry and academia to work together in building up knowledge, exploring and experimenting, including through joint research and development programs. In this regard, governments can also provide space for new concepts to be tested and realized through flexible — rather than restrictive — regulations, for example, by designating certain projects or districts as regulatory sandboxes to facilitate new ideas. This approach was taken in the development of Singapore's first — and perhaps the world's largest — underground district cooling system at Marina Bay, where the use of the system was mandated by an Act of Parliament and regulated by the government's Energy Market Authority.

How cities advance the use of underground space depends on their particular needs, levels of technological capability and societal acceptance. The cities that do this well will be the ones whose governments embrace imagination, are willing to push boundaries, bring stakeholders and experts together and empower experimentation with "wild ideas."

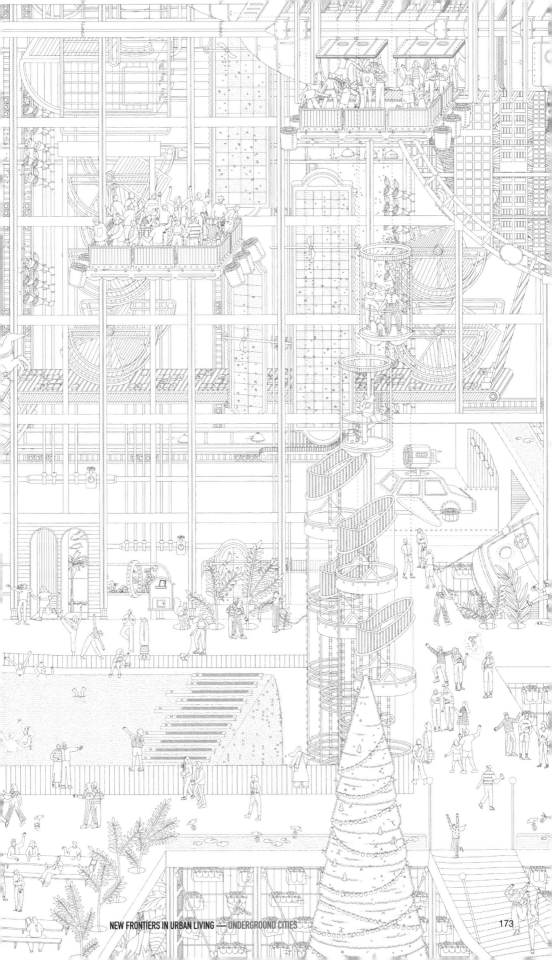

HONG KONG: A MATTER OF WHEN, NOT IF OR HOW

John Endicott, AECOM

To me, the underground is — and always has been — a place of beauty, excitement and security. I have long had a fascination with what lies below ground. I guess I must have inherited it from my distant Paleolithic ancestors who ventured deep into caves and painted beautiful depictions of now extinct animals.

As a child, I discovered a small natural cave in an abandoned quarry where rock had been mined to build farm cottages. It had thin stalactites hanging from the roof and shorter, fatter stalagmites located immediately below, patiently catching the drips of mineral-rich water as they fell. I would work my way into the darkness, candle stub in hand, the small flame casting patterns on the glittering rock coated in a thin pale-pink film of calcium carbonate. Later, as a treat, I was taken to Kent's Cavern in Torquay, which the Victorians had discovered and set up as a show cave, with meandering passages, fine mosses and ferns that grew around the electric lights. I saw the fossilized skull of a saber-toothed carnivore, embedded in the roof of the cave for millions of years.

My childhood home had three stories above ground and a basement. Going to bed on a moonlit winter's night, I was afraid of being chased up the stairs by some bogeyman. The basement, on the other hand, was the home of a coal-fired boiler, warm and cozy, with a heap of coal and kindling and all kinds of remnant treasures stored in case somebody wanted them someday. Fascinated by caves, it was a natural step for me to train in both geotechnical and structural disciplines as a ground engineer.

174

Hong Kong's Evolution

Because of that training, I was lucky enough to be invited to Hong Kong in 1975 to work on the design of two underground railway stations and two tunnels. Since then, it has been my home for more than 40 years.

Over the course of those four decades, I have seen Hong Kong undergo a metamorphosis. When I first arrived, streets were congested, sewage was discharged directly into the harbor and the water supply was uncertain. Yet today, Hong Kong is a globally important financial center and vibrant modern region. It has achieved this level of growth with few natural advantages beyond its geographical location in the fast developing Greater Bay Area and its natural deepwater harbor, one of the best in the world. Hong Kong's achievement is doubly remarkable given the engineering challenges posed by its steep terrain and the scarcity of land. The territory covers just 1,000km^2. Accepting the natural limits imposed by the mountainous topography, an ordinance of 1976 designated half the land area as country parks. When you include the military reserves that are closed to the public, the portion of land that is conserved — and therefore undevelopable — rises to around two-thirds.

With land scarce and water in short supply, the main motors for Hong Kong's development have been its industrious and enterprising people, along with the engineering prowess that has enabled the infrastructure that supports them.

The Role of Infrastructure in Accommodating High-density Living

A driving force for the expansion of infrastructure in Hong Kong
has been population growth, from a low of 600,000 inhabitants
immediately after the Second World War to four million in the 1970s
and more than seven million today. I have long been impressed by
the sheer number of people crowded into a small territory — their
means of coexistence, along with their energy and determination to
get things done.

Providing adequate housing for the large and increasing population
has been an ongoing challenge. Given the limited availability of land,
most buildings for housing, offices, hotels and even industrial use are
high-rise, and getting taller all the time. If buildings up to 20 floors

below: The construction of mass housing provided permanent accommodation for Hong
Kong's rapidly growing population in the postwar years. Here, future resettlement dwellers
are housed in a transit camp alongside a new Kwun Tong estate, 1966. Photo HKSARG

above: Before the construction of the cross-harbor road tunnel, vehicle ferries were a common sight in Hong Kong waters. Photo HKSARG

right: Approach to cross-harbor tunnel shortly after completion in 1972. © Heather Coulson/ University of Hong Kong Libraries

were common early in the 1970s, heights now exceed 80 stories. Much of the public housing is about 40 stories and closely packed together, resulting in high density. Because of the steep terrain, developments follow the corridors of low-lying land. Urban sprawl is limited to former farmland and villages in the New Territories.

Dubbed "a barren rock" in the 1840s, Hong Kong has become a leader in first-class, reliable infrastructure, enhancing its livability despite the intensive development of its urban areas. Many elements of this infrastructure lie underground, most notably the city's mass transit system which accounts for more than 42 percent of total passenger trips in the city.

Laying the Groundwork for the Mass Transit Railway

Before the opening of the first cross-harbor road tunnel and the mass transit railway (MTR), the only way to cross the inner harbor was by ferry — a very time-consuming exercise that the wealthy managed to circumvent by keeping two cars, one on each side of the harbor, and employing two drivers: a "Hong Kong driver" and a "Kowloon driver," respectively. As the tunnel absorbed the car traffic, the use of ferries declined and sampans were no longer needed to scull late-night revelers home. But not everyone was so quick to adapt. When I first arrived and could only afford to live in the rural area, my older cousin living on Hong Kong Island was reluctant to visit, insisting "But John, it would take all day to drive out to see you."

The first fixed crossing of the harbor was a long time coming. In 1948 Sir Patrick Abercrombie included a proposal for a crossing as part of his work on the strategic plan for Hong Kong. This was four years

LOOKING FORWARD

after he drew up his plan for the reconstruction of Greater London after the war. Indeed, for Abercrombie, a crossing was the plan's "biggest single planning and engineering feature." It was "something much more than an underground traffic link," conceived as "a symbol of the unity of interests" of Hong Kong and the UK.[1] But it would be another 20 years before work got underway. Symbol of unity or not, there was the problem of cost and the tunnel was ultimately constructed under a 30-year private-sector franchise based on a build-operate-transfer model. Within 15 minutes of opening, over 700 vehicles had driven through the tunnel. Within three and a half years, revenue from tolls had recovered the construction costs.

Increasing road congestion provided part of the impetus for the launch of the MTR. With years of experience in building tunnels for road, rail and water supply, from the steam-driven Kowloon–Canton Railway in the late 1800s to the cross-harbor road tunnel connecting Kowloon and Hong Kong Island in 1972, the local construction industry paved the way. The original plan was for a three-line system with about 25 underground stations and three stations above ground. A Mitsubishi-led consortium was due to undertake the work, but the OPEC oil embargo intervened. After construction costs doubled within the space of six months, the consortium exercised an option to withdraw from the contract in December 1974. The government was left with little leeway. While the territory had grown increasingly prosperous, its ability to raise funds was hampered by the uncertainty of its future — the UK's lease was set to expire in 1997.

A decision was made to test the market with a much reduced scheme, a Modified Initial System (MIS) of one railway line with 15 stations that would run from Kwun Tong, with a depot in the industrial area of Kowloon Bay, connecting densely populated Kowloon to the business district of Central on Hong Kong Island. The route included Mong Kok, then the most densely occupied urban area in the world. Along Nathan Road, the spine of Kowloon, the average density of 130,000 people per square kilometer suggested that each station would be used by something in the order of 60,000 people per day, which justified eight-car trains running at two-minute intervals. The MIS was divided into packages, typically comprised of a single station or a single tunnel between stations. Tenders for some contracts were invited from overseas companies with prior experience constructing underground railways, while others were reserved for local contractors.

Birth of the MTR
In 1975 the Paul Y Construction Co Ltd (Paul Y) invited me to Hong Kong to prepare a contractor's tender design for the underground railway system. I helped to prepare tenders for five packages of the MTR. These were for three underground stations (Wong Tai Sin, Diamond Hill and Choi Hung), cut and cover tunnels from Diamond Hill Station to Choi Hung Station, and a bored tunnel from Choi Hung Station going towards Kowloon Bay.[2] Not only was Paul Y's offer technically sound and innovative, but the tendered prices were lower than the engineer's estimates — a great signal that the MIS would be viable.

above: The MTR's first day, October 1, 1979. Photos © South China Morning Post

above: The first MTR line, inaugurated in 1979, connected the business district of Central on Hong Kong Island with densely populated Kowloon and the industrial area of Kowloon Bay. Photo South China Morning Post

From its inauguration in 1979, the first MTR line was popular and heavily used. The success of the initial system led to the construction of the Tsuen Wan Line, running north from Central, through densely populated Kowloon, and into the New Territories. Tsuen Wan (along with Tuen Mun and Sha Tin in the New Territories) was one of the first generation of new towns developed in a 10-year housing program (1973–83) that aimed to provide permanent accommodation for around 1.8 million people. To relieve pressure on the densely developed urban areas in Kowloon and on Hong Kong Island, the new housing was concentrated in the New Territories, which were then still largely rural.

High-density development along corridors is ideal for mass transit, yielding high patronage. Such was the density along the route that during rush hour one could queue for as many as three trains just to squeeze in. With limited space at ground level, most of the MIS was underground, relieving congestion on the roads and pavement above.

MTR Funding

The Hong Kong Government funded the first underground railway line, recognizing that the clear advantages of providing low-cost public transport outweighed the financial burden of building it. So great was the demand that the line paid for itself in six years. The next lines to be built were in less densely populated areas with less patronage, so loans were obtained from the international market. An alternative funding model was tried out with the subsequent Island Line, which serves the north shore of Hong Kong Island. The air rights above all eight stations were put up for auction, raising HK$8 billion, a substantial portion of the construction costs. Other cities have now adopted this financial model, bringing the construction of an underground metro within their reach. Singapore, Taipei, Bangkok,

below: The MTR's pioneering approach to co-development, making use of the space above underground stations, began with Telford Gardens, built on top on top of the Kowloon Bay depot in 1980. Photo AECOM

Delhi, Kolkata, Chennai, and now Hanoi and Jakarta — all have built metro systems in this way, just to mention the projects in which I have personally been involved.

Hong Kong's pioneering use of co-development, utilizing the space above underground railway stations, has been a hallmark feature from the beginning. Telford Gardens, the first such development, was completed in 1980. Located on top of the depot at Kowloon Bay, it consists of 41 residential blocks housing almost 5,000 flats.

The world's largest TBM — at 17.63m in diameter — was deployed in the excavation of the subsea link between Tuen Mun and Hong Kong-Zhuhai-Macao Bridge Hong Kong Port. Photo HKSARG

Adjacent to it is an office tower containing the MTRC headquarters and a shopping plaza with 250 stores. More recently, the high-rise towers that form an iconic gateway to the harbor — the 88-floor IFC and 108-floor ICC — have been built above the MTR airport express services at Hong Kong Station and Kowloon Station respectively. Mixed-use co-development has made the MTR one of the most profitable metro systems in the world.

Connecting the many different nodes of urban density that make up Hong Kong, the MTR network of 156 stations now extends over 218km and carries more than five million people every day. With a 90-second headway between trains, the MTRC's aim is "lift within two minutes, train within three minutes." Intensively used, it recovers some 185 percent of its operating costs through fares — a far greater proportion than any other rail network in the world — and reinvests the surplus in capital expansion and upgrades. The MTR is recognized worldwide as a gold standard in transit management, showing that pedestrian mobility can be clean, cool and comfortable below ground.

Construction Aspects
In the relatively quiet areas of Diamond Hill and Choi Hung, I was able to see Paul Y build two MTR stations without any technical problems. In the more congested areas, however, construction was not without its difficulties. Using the cut and cover method to build underground stations that were themselves almost as wide as the streets in the central business district necessarily caused disruption, even when half of the station site was covered with temporary decking to permit a limited flow of traffic and pedestrians.

Inevitably, construction encountered geotechnical challenges as well. In 1976, for example, excavations for underground stations in Mong Kok District went below the water table and the resulting seepage caused subsidence in the adjacent properties. Hong Kong has continuously honed its techniques, however, broadening its repertoire from the drill and blast mining methods of the earlier era to the use of Tunnel Boring Machines (TBMs), which can be adapted to deal with all kinds of ground conditions, from weak soils to very hard rock.

Most of the railway tunnels in Hong Kong have been bored beneath the ground using TBMs. Barring mishaps, these can achieve faster rates of advance, minimize surface disturbance in near-surface applications and even work at great depths below water, where it is neither practical nor safe for mining workers to operate. In fact, the world's largest TBM — at 17.63m in diameter — was deployed in the excavation of the subsea link between Tuen Mun and Hong Kong-Zhuhai-Macao Bridge Hong Kong Port, which has twin tunnels —

each with a two-lane carriageway. A hyperbaric chamber attached to the TBM allowed experienced manpower to work under compressed air, similar to deep sea diving conditions. The project also pioneered the use of robotic arm to change some of the cutters located in the pressurized chamber, reducing the need for manpower to work within the compressed air environment.

Hong Kong's world-renowned expertise in tunneling has delivered railways and roads, water supply, stormwater drainage and wastewater sewers, gas mains and electric cables that are integrated into the fabric of the city and make full use of its developable land. Studies are currently underway for more extensive uses of its underground spaces.

Current Use of the Underground
The topography and geology of Hong Kong are well suited to the development of man-made caverns. The steep terrain allows access tunnels to be driven horizontally into the ground, and there is an abundance of strong igneous rocks, such as granite, which are often sufficiently massive to be self-supporting. Moreover, the scarcity and extremely high cost of developable land justifies the expense of excavating the caverns.

Since 1990 the Government of Hong Kong has carried out a series of planning studies for creating underground space, with a focus on accommodating facilities that are difficult to locate on the surface —

either because their function is not welcome or because of a shortage of land. The first significant outcome was the underground sewage treatment works for a population of 35,000 at Stanley, constructed in two caverns in 1995. Subsequently, other caverns have been constructed and put into use — seven of them as MTR stations.[3] Caverns at Kau Shat Wan on Lantau provide secure storage for explosives. As a result of its underground location, the Island West Refuse Transfer Station contains odors and keeps the heaps of refuse out of public view. The Western Salt Water Service Reservoirs have replaced surface reservoirs, releasing much-needed land for expansion of the University of Hong Kong.

The recently completed West Kowloon Station (WKS) of the high speed rail system connecting Hong Kong and Mainland China was built in a deep excavation some 200m wide, 30m deep and 660m long — nearly ten times the volume of the eight-car underground railway stations that are typical for the MTR in Hong Kong. Passengers are transported seamlessly between Hong Kong and neighboring cities in Guangdong province through dedicated tunnels which are part of the largest high-speed rail network in the world. From the point of arrival, some 30m below ground, there is a smooth, high-capacity access through immigration and customs traveling in both directions. There are large open areas for greeting and interchange with other means of transportation conveniently located in the heart of the harbor area.

One of the crowning glories of the station, however, is its roof, which draws natural light into the underground layers of the station and also serves as a rooftop park. In the daytime, the generous underground spaces are lit naturally from roof lights and the station is of course fully air-conditioned, warm in winter and cool in summer. The design is entirely people-oriented. The columns supporting the high-rise development above the station are hidden from view, passing seamlessly through the interior.

Future Use of the Underground

Having been extensively involved with underground development, I was invited to be a member of the Town Planning Board in Hong Kong. Developing caverns was on the back-burner when I joined, but Hong Kong had an extensive program for urban renewal. Outdated city blocks were purchased, cleared and used for integrated development, including several floors of basement and subway connections to the MTR. A recent example of urban renewal to be carried forward is Langham Place in Mong Kok, with restaurants and shops many floors below ground and pedestrian subways to the nearby MTR station. Also underway are focused studies for development beneath open spaces like Kowloon Park and Victoria Park that envisage improvements to the open-air facilities, such as swimming pools and tennis courts, as well as spaces for the elderly to simply put their feet up and watch the world go by.

Other strategic surveys have mapped out locations with ready vehicular access and good rock for mining caverns, including former quarries with exposed rock slopes. Already, one pragmatic outcome is the proposed relocation of the Sha Tin sewage treatment works, which serves about one million people but has reached capacity, with no room for further expansion. The existing works, with its many open tanks, spreads over some 25ha. A value-capture exercise indicated that the vacated site would be prime building land. There are good views towards the Sha Tin Racecourse on one side and a beautiful unspoiled marine channel on the other. Its sale would raise enough money to pay for newly upgraded treatment works.

Across the marine channel from the sewage plant is a range of steep hills composed of Cretaceous granite, one of the better rocks in Hong Kong for constructing caverns. The rock quality and location provide potential for some 65 caverns, with connecting adits and a shaft for ventilation. During the public consultations in the preliminary design phase, some residents voiced objections, alarmed by the word "sewage" and the prospect of any form of construction. In fact, the relocation of the facility would remove the unsightly and malodorous exposed tanks that have blighted the landscape for 40 years. On the surface, the only evidence of the new works would be two portals — one for general access and one for other services. For a major project such as this, the total time from initial concept study to the commissioning of the new plant and decommissioning of the old plant with site clean-up will be in the order of 30 years. Strategic planning for major projects has to anticipate needs decades in advance and incorporate an increased awareness of the benefits of underground construction.

Engineering the Future

Currently there are about seven million people on 500km² of developable land in Hong Kong. There is potential for an equivalent amount beneath our feet — a reserve of space that could accommodate anything or any activity that does not need "its back to the sun."

At the same time, a 252-story building is under construction and poised to set a record as the world's tallest building. When constructed, the Jeddah Tower will surpass the Burj Khalifa by 72m. Just as buildings reaching 1,000m into the sky are entirely feasible these days from a technical standpoint, so are buildings — even cities — burrowing 252 stories below ground. The techniques are available to enable the work to be done and they provide endless new possibilities for high-density and space-constrained cities to tap subterranean space as another form of land utilization.

Far from being in the realm of science fiction, these ideas are based on the sensible science of civil engineering. We have barely scratched the surface (so to speak) of the world beneath our feet. As my journey together with Hong Kong has consistently impressed on me, the capability is there, subject to the desire and the funding.

To me, the possibility of living, working, playing and learning below ground is as exciting as ever and if I am alive when the day comes, I will be first in the queue to buy a flat below Conduit Road on Hong Kong Island.

below: Victoria Harbor skyline.
Photo fanjianhua/Shutterstock.com

SINGAPORE'S NEXT FRONTIER: GOING UNDERGROUND

Urban Redevelopment Authority of Singapore

Singapore is a small island. With a land area of about 725km^2 — one-half the size of Greater London or one-third of the Tokyo metropolitan area — it must support the varied needs of both a sovereign nation and a city of 5.7 million people.

These needs include housing and schools, offices and industrial estates, major infrastructure, such as reservoirs, a port and an airport, as well as national defense. As it has developed, Singapore has pursued the concurrent goals of supporting economic growth, enhancing environmental quality and strengthening social resilience. To ensure there is sufficient capacity to cater for future growth and opportunities, while maintaining a good quality of life, it takes a long-term approach in planning land use.

The Concept Plan plays an important role in balancing Singapore's multiple land-use needs. First mapped out in 1971, and reviewed regularly, it sets the direction for land use and transport strategies over the next 40 to 50 years, anticipating changing social and economic needs. These broad strategies are translated into more detailed plans in the Master Plan, a statutory land-use plan that guides Singapore's physical development for the next 10 to 15 years.

As a city-state with nowhere to sprawl, Singapore has used various means to overcome its shortage of land, including land reclamation, building upwards (within the bounds of airport height limits), co-locating uses and recycling land for more productive uses. The next frontier in this quest to increase Singapore's land and space capacity is going underground.

Going Underground

Underground development is a strategic resource that many cities capitalize on, both to create large amounts of additional space within densely populated urban areas and to provide stable environments for uses that require high levels of physical protection and climate control. For well over a century, cities such as New York and London have had substantial underground networks for transport and

above: Marina Barrage, completed in 2008, forms a tidal barrier and freshwater reservoir while also providing a space for outdoor activities.
Photo DoctorEgg via Getty Images

North-South Line and East-West Line
Singapore's first MRT tunnels

Central Expressway
Chin Swee Tunnel and Kampong Java Tunnel are Singapore's first road tunnels

Woodlands Bus Interchange
Singapore's first underground bus interchange

CityLink Mall
Singapore's first fully underground shopping mall

1985   87   89   1990   96

Note: Estimated completion timeline for future projects

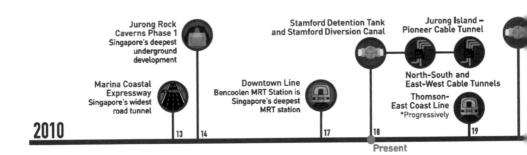

Jurong Rock Caverns Phase 1
Singapore's deepest underground development

Stamford Detention Tank and Stamford Diversion Canal

Jurong Island – Pioneer Cable Tunnel

Marina Coastal Expressway
Singapore's widest road tunnel

Downtown Line
Bencoolen MRT Station is Singapore's deepest MRT station

North-South and East-West Cable Tunnels

Thomson-East Coast Line
*Progressively

2010   13   14   17   18   19

Present

above: Timeline of Singapore's underground development.
© Urban Redevelopment Authority

utilities. Some cities, such as Montreal and Tokyo, have extensive basement developments for pedestrian connectivity. Others, such as Helsinki and Hong Kong, have gone beyond the common uses of underground space, building caverns to house facilities such as reservoirs and storage.

The exploration of underground space is not something new in Singapore either. In 1965, the year it gained independence, the first large-scale underground car park opened at Raffles Place. Utility cables were also moved underground to improve the streetscape, joining other utilities such as water and sewer pipes. Underground Mass Rapid Transit (MRT) tracks and stations followed in the 1980s, along with underpasses. A deep tunnel sewage system was introduced in the 1990s. Many private buildings now also have basements to accommodate retail spaces and car parks. Deeper underground, Singapore has Southeast Asia's first underground caverns for oil storage, and the world's most advanced underground ammunition facility.

Optimizing use of land and space, improving the quality of the living environment by freeing up land on the surface for more people-centric uses, enhancing connectivity, and increasing the resilience of infrastructure — these are the four key objectives of Singapore's use of its underground space.

North East Line
Singapore's first
fully underground
MRT line

Opera Estate
Detention
Tank

01

03

Marina Bay Common
Services Tunnel Phase 1
Southeast Asia's
first multi-utility tunnel

Kallang-Paya Lebar
Expressway
Southeast Asia's longest
underground road tunnel

Underground
Ammunition Facility
Singapore s first
cavern development

Deep Tunnel
Sewerage
System Phase 1

08

Kim Chuan Depot
World's first
underground train depot

Circle Line
The Bras Basah Station
on Circle Line features
the longest escalator
in the whole MRT system

09

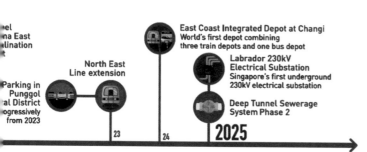

...el
...na East
...lination

...Parking in
Punggol
...al District
...ogressively
from 2023

North East
Line extension

23

24

East Coast Integrated Depot at Changi
World's first depot combining
three train depots and one bus depot

Labrador 230kV
Electrical Substation
Singapore's first underground
230kV electrical substation

Deep Tunnel Sewerage
System Phase 2

2025

Managing Underground Space

Going underground has its challenges. Underground infrastructure, particularly when it forms part of a network, involves multiple land uses across different land strata, some of them in public ownership, some of them private. A high level of coordination is required among the different stakeholders — government agencies as well as private landowners and developers — to resolve the resulting issues of land and space ownership, property management, planning and building control.

The safety of underground construction and its potential impact on surface developments are also important concerns. Excavating and constructing underground infrastructure may unavoidably disrupt surface activities. Underground projects are often costlier (at least in terms of the initial investment required) and more time-consuming to construct than similar projects above ground. When there is a lack of information on the underground space, higher risks are also involved.

All these challenges mean that there is a need to move away from the traditional project-led approach, where underground spaces are allocated on a first-come, first-served basis. Like other cities, such as Hong Kong and Helsinki, which have holistically reviewed the potential of their underground space, Singapore is moving towards a more systematic plan-led approach.

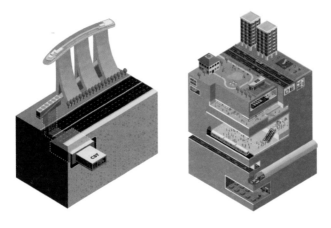

left: The district cooling system at Marina Bay. right: Placing utilities
and transport underground frees up much-needed space on the surface.
Images © Urban Redevelopment Authority

Clear Legislation

Who owns the space beneath the city is a key question that needs
to be considered in developing a long-term planning framework. The
answer varies according to where you are in the world. In Helsinki
the private landowner's right to use underground space is generally
limited to the shallowest 6m beneath a piece of land. In London, by
contrast, property law generally remains rooted in a Latin dictum,
Cuius est solum eius est usque ad coelum et ad inferos, which
mandates that the owners of the surface land have rights to all the
space above and beneath it, "up to the Heavens and down to Hell."
While regulations allow for exceptions, for the extraction of mineral
or water resources, for example, the right of access beneath private
properties for third-party development is often not well defined.

Singapore's legislative and land administration framework is
constantly reviewed to keep up with the times. To facilitate long-
term planning, the State Lands Act was amended in 2015 to
provide clarity on the ownership and use of underground space.
The boundary of surface-land ownership today extends to 30m
below the Singapore Height Datum (SHD), a depth that is assessed
to be reasonably sufficient for the surface landowner's use and
enjoyment.[1] The foundations of a development may extend beyond
this limit if it is deemed necessary for structural stability. While
supporting the rights of landowners, the change in regulation allows
the State to make use of the deep underground space, for example,
in the form of caverns if required.

As the city becomes more built up, there may be a need for some
public infrastructure to run underneath private developments
at depths that are still within private ownership. In the past this

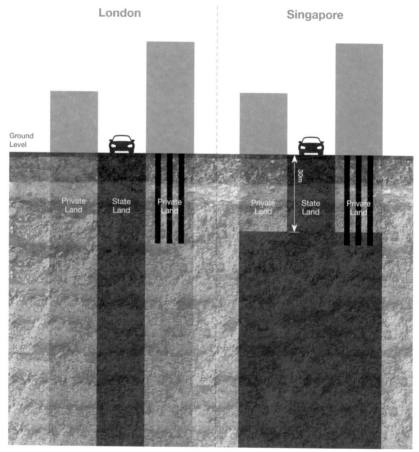

above: In Singapore the boundary of surface land ownership extends to 30m below the Singapore Height Datum, in contrast with other cities where land ownership is not so clearly defined. © Urban Redevelopment Authority

above: Photogrammetry technology is being used to create photo-realistic models of mass rapid transit tunnels from the inside. © Land Transport Authority/GovTech

would have entailed either using easement rights where possible or acquiring the entire plot of land, including the surface use, even if it was unaffected by the underground infrastructure. The Land Acquisition Act was amended to allow Government to acquire just the specific stratum of space required for the public projects, without affecting the surface land.

Underground Data

Data plays a significant role in urban planning. Traditionally, planning data includes population demographics, zoning plans, topography and environmental factors. Planning the underground requires a whole raft of additional data sets — not just on underground ownership, but on geology, underground structures, foundations and utilities.

In many densely built-up cities, however, information on what has been put underground over the years is often patchy or highly inaccurate, complicating the process of underground planning and development. Extensive survey work may be needed to identify underground infrastructure and, even then, the start of construction can turn up unwelcome surprises that cause project delays and cost overruns.

To overcome this, Singapore is exploring ways to map the underground space in a more productive and effective manner. One such initiative is a joint effort by the Singapore-ETH Center to establish best-practice guidelines and technologies as the basis for creating a reliable 3D map of underground utility networks in Singapore.

Singapore is also exploring the use of photogrammetry technology to create photo-realistic 3D models of the MRT tunnels from the inside,

above: Mapping the underground. 3D model of the geology of Singapore.
© Building & Construction Authority. below: 3D digital rendering of utility
networks. © Singapore Land Authority, Singapore-ETH Center

which could then potentially be used to create a 3D model of the external geometry to represent the actual tunnel structures.

Establishing best practices for capturing information on future infrastructure can ensure that future generations will not face the challenges of today. For larger infrastructure and building structures, planners can now extract the necessary information — for example, on the external geometry of the structure with proper geospatial references — using 3D Building Information Modeling (BIM).

As this database of building information in 3D is built up, it will show the location of basements, piles and foundations to guide future development.

For shallow utility lines, standards have been developed to ensure that the information captured by surveys can be used to generate 3D models automatically. These Utility Survey Standards will improve the accuracy of as-built data and ultimately achieve a homogenous utility database to support planning and decision-making.

In addition to knowing where things are underground, it is also crucial to understand the geological characteristics of the ground, because this influences the construction method and structural design, which in turn affect construction time and cost. The more geological information available, the more precise the construction design can be.

Knowing the geology is particularly important in the planning of caverns, which are typically constructed in good quality rocks, to ensure that the structure can be self-supporting. Singapore currently has two cavern developments: Jurong Rock Caverns and the Underground Ammunition Facility. Combined, these two facilities have freed up about 360ha of land, equivalent to more than 510 football pitches. Given the potential for significant land savings, this is an area that is being actively explored for further development.

Singapore is made up of five major types of rock and soil formations in addition to reclaimed land. The characteristics vary significantly across the different types of geology, with very different geological conditions often occurring over a small area. Within the same type of rock, the strength can vary due to faults, fractures and other natural processes. This presents challenges in construction as engineers often have to cater for different types of geology and soil characteristics within a single project.

Since it was set up in 2010, the Singapore Geology Office has carried out detailed geological surveys and investigations in selected areas, to build on the available information. Boreholes up to 200m deep are drilled to obtain ground samples and the findings are then used to develop a 3D geological model that shows in greater detail the formations, their interfaces and the presence of any faults or fractures.

The value of accurate underground data is increased when it is shared with the engineering and construction industry, academia and the general public. Where possible, the Geology Office makes publicly available the geological information obtained during the implementation of public sector projects. There are also ongoing efforts to make the process of obtaining information more streamlined by creating a central portal for shallow utilities.

Jurong Rock Caverns *(Teo Tiong Yong, JTC Corporation)*
Most of Singapore's subterranean infrastructure lies at a maximum depth of 70m. Located 150m below the ground — and 130m beneath the seabed — Jurong Rock Caverns (JRC) are the city-state's deepest underground works to date. To realize this hugely challenging project, JTC Corporation (JTC), the state-owned entity responsible for industrial infrastructure development, collaborated with a large international team of specialists, including some 280 engineers.

The team employed a variety of construction techniques, including the drill and blast method, to build two access shafts, five nine-story caverns for the storage of liquid hydrocarbons, and 9km of tunnels, along with supporting utilities, such as a wastewater treatment plant, various valves and pumping systems, and a vapor recovery unit. During the 11 years of construction, some 3.5 million cubic meters of rock were removed. Now complete, the caverns have a capacity of 1.47 million cubic meters — a volume equivalent to 600 Olympic-sized swimming pools.

Planning works started early in 2001, with a site investigation and feasibility study, and intensified in 2006 when in-principle approval was sought from the relevant state authorities for the Environmental Impact (EIA) and Quantitative Risk (QRA) Assessments. Anticipating that the main contractor could find it difficult to secure the necessary insurance cover, given the scale of the project and the risks involved, JTC also engaged an insurance broker to review owner-procured insurance coverage at an early stage.

The drill and blast method entails the use of large quantities of explosives. Transporting these from the commercial storage facilities on the mainland to Jurong Island, a special security zone, would have been immensely difficult and time-consuming. After engaging with the relevant state authorities, JTC obtained in-principle approval

Jurong Rock Caverns are located 150m below the ground, and 130m below the seabed. © JTC

to construct engineered explosive storage houses on Jurong Island itself. This made it possible to plan a more aggressive timeline — 24 hours a day, seven days a week — for completing the excavation of the tunnels and caverns.

Any excavation runs the risk of encountering unforeseen ground conditions that could give rise to contractual disputes and delay the project. Located within the Jurong Formation, which consists of sedimentary rocks, JRC had its fair share of unpredictable ground conditions and water seepage as a result of the non-homogeneous nature of the rocks. To manage these unforeseen elements, it was decided to adopt a shared-risk approach between JTC and the contractor for the excavation. A report documenting the baseline ground conditions for the excavation work was prepared. Provisional quantities for the rock reinforcement, including the rock bolts, shotcrete and grouting works, were included in the tender. While JTC would pay for all necessary rock reinforcement work, the contractor had to propose and take responsibility for the rates at which this reinforcement would be installed. Any technical dispute relating to the works would be referred to a Dispute Resolution Board, jointly appointed by JTC and the contractor.

To keep geological surprises to a minimum, extensive ground surveys were carried out before embarking on the design. During construction, deep investigation holes up to 60m long were bored to verify the rock conditions, while 15m-deep probe holes were systematically used to check water ingress before the start of any excavation work. When excessive groundwater was detected, a pressurized pre-grouting up to 15m ahead of the tunnel face was performed. A high-pressure mixture of water and cement, the grouting flows into the cracks, joints and fissures of the rocks and then seals them up as it hardens.

The caverns are designed to be unlined and located well below the groundwater table, which is unprecedented in Singapore. The hydraulic containment principle utilizes the principle of pressure difference between the water saturating the rock mass around the caverns and the pressure inside the caverns. As a precautionary measure, water curtain galleries, consisting of 6m-wide tunnels with 80m-long boreholes drilled at intervals of 10m, were provided to enhance the hydraulic pressure outside the caverns.

During construction, the water curtain galleries were kept at atmospheric pressure and the water curtain boreholes were injected with water individually and in advance of cavern excavation to keep the rock mass saturated. During operation, the galleries and the boreholes are both injected with water and maintained at a pressure of 10 bar, determined during the design phase. The injection of water in the water curtain galleries/boreholes improves the gradient distribution of the hydraulic pressure in the rock mass, keeping the stored product safely within the caverns.

As the water pressure outside the caverns is greater than the pressure inside the caverns, groundwater seeps through the cavern walls. It is pumped out automatically and treated above ground at the wastewater treatment plant before being discharged into the sea.

Robust Planning Policies and Processes

Underground space is a resource that should be planned in a holistic way, in tandem with the space above ground. In planning new areas, Singapore's planners look at how the underground could be used to enhance the whole urban environment by optimizing land, for example, and improving connectivity by putting infrastructure underground.

Part of this underground space includes caverns that can only be created in locations where the rock is of good quality and accessible. In Singapore's case, this is more likely in the central and western regions. The potential use of such cavern spaces must be compatible with the above-ground and surrounding uses.

Given the many competing demands for underground spaces — including MRT tunnels, pedestrian links and utility tunnels — a hierarchy is set to determine which underground use has priority in a specific stratum of space. In general, people-centric uses are located at shallower depths, while utility-related uses are deeper. This hierarchy helps to organize the underground space, increasing connectivity between developments while reducing the potential for conflicts, especially within the more congested layers of shallower underground space.

Careful consideration is also given to the planning and design of vertical access points to create smooth connections between the underground facilities, the developments they serve and the environment above ground.

USE/CIRCULATION
PEDESTRIAN

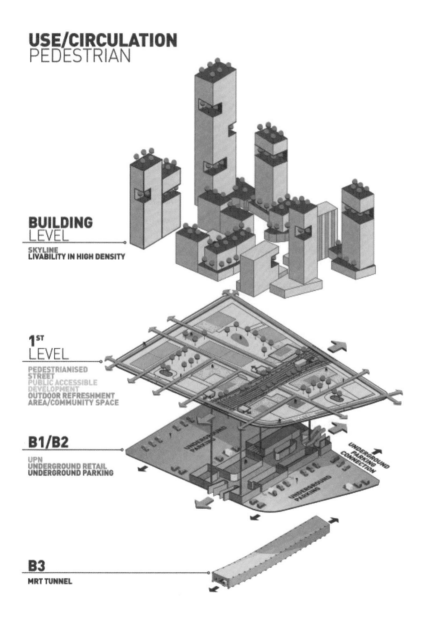

BUILDING
LEVEL

SKYLINE
LIVABILITY IN HIGH DENSITY

1ST
LEVEL

PEDESTRIANISED
STREET
PUBLIC ACCESSIBLE
DEVELOPMENT
**OUTDOOR REFRESHMENT
AREA/COMMUNITY SPACE**

B1/B2

UPN
UNDERGROUND RETAIL
UNDERGROUND PARKING

B3

MRT TUNNEL

Marina Bay and the Common Services Tunnel

The Marina Bay area is a great example of Singapore's integrated approach to the planning and use of underground spaces. An extension of the downtown core, it allows for the expansion of the existing central business district (CBD) — covering a total area of around 360ha. It is about nine times the size of London's Canary Wharf. But Marina Bay is not just a financial and business center; it is also a civic space and a community playground.

Put in place by the Singapore Government, the Common Services Tunnel (CST) is state-of-the-art infrastructure to support the sustainable development of Marina Bay. It houses and distributes key utilities including potable water, NEWater, chilled water for air-conditioning, electricity and telecommunication services.[2] After Japan, Singapore is the second country in Asia to implement a comprehensive CST network on this scale. Construction of the first phase began in 1998, after a multi-year study to evaluate its benefits and costs. To date, about 5.7km of the network has been completed.

The CST offers many benefits over conventional methods of laying utility services under the road carriageway or service verges. Service reliability and security are improved because pipes and cables can be regularly inspected and maintained. The concrete tunnel structures also provide greater protection against accidental damage from nearby excavations. Since no roadworks are required to lay, repair or maintain utility services, there is less noise and traffic disruption when additional cables and pipes are installed to serve new developments. Valuable surface land is also released for development, because a portion of the road verges is no longer needed for the laying of underground utilities.

In addition, the CST network facilitates the implementation of district-wide systems. The district cooling system conveys chilled water to all developments in Marina Bay for air-conditioning, removing the need for unsightly facilities such as cooling towers and condensers. Rooftop utility spaces can now be transformed into gardens or outdoor refreshment areas instead. Besides achieving water and energy savings through economies of scale, the system reduces the amount of space needed for an air-conditioning plant room within each individual development. The heat from the district cooling plant is fed back into the Marina Bay Sands hotel development for heating water. Provisions have also been made within the CST for the future installation of a district pneumatic refuse conveyance system to remove waste underground through suction pipes. By eliminating the need for rubbish trucks to call at each development, the system will improve the overall living environment.

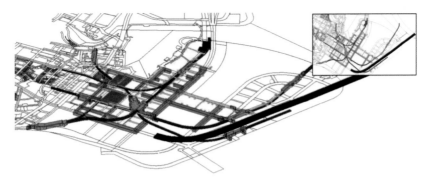

above: 3D model of Marina Bay development.
© Urban Redevelopment Authority

The development of such a massive and complex underground project required close teamwork among government agencies and private developers, as well as skillful coordination and innovative thinking to ensure the different phases of the project were completed in time to supply utilities to new developments. During the excavation phase, the ground conditions of Marina Bay posed a particular challenge. The geology — reclaimed land underlaid with a thick layer of soft marine clay — was complicated further by the presence of long-forgotten buried structures, including a lighters' wharf, pier foundations and, most significantly, a seawall or rock mole from the early 1900s that was 1.5km long, 30m deep, 60m wide and formed of rocks as heavy as 20 metric tons. The submerged mole had to be removed because it formed a barrier to the installation of pile foundations and temporary retaining structures. But removing the earth covering the mole using the conventional dry excavation method would have been a logistical nightmare. The innovative solution was to deploy a flooded cofferdam instead. Over a period of six years, the structure was progressively dismantled, with GPS being used to ensure no remnant rocks were left behind. To minimize the delay in the works, the CST project had to take on a compressed timeline, with more parallel activities and extended working hours.

In addition to the CST network, underground space also serves to enhance connectivity in Marina Bay, which is currently served by four different underground MRT lines, with a fifth under construction. Central to the vision of a pedestrian-friendly city center, where people can move around seamlessly and in all-weather comfort, is the development of a comprehensive underground pedestrian network that links basements of developments with nearby MRT stations and public amenities such as the waterfront and parks.

The network will be progressively extended as government land sale conditions require each new development to connect into it. A good example is the Marina Bay Financial Center, which opened in 2013. The site provides a crucial link to the existing CBD via basement-level walkways that connect with adjacent buildings, including The Sail and One Raffles Quay, as well as two MRT stations (Raffles Place and Downtown), and lead to other key areas such as the waterfront promenade. Knock-out panels were also safeguarded to support linkages to future developments. Part of the network is an underground mall with retail and dining. Pedestrians can come up to the surface at various access points using escalators and lifts.

The different underground uses in the Marina Bay area again observe the hierarchy where people-centric uses are shallower and utility-related uses deeper. The levels of the pedestrian network are kept constant as far as possible, minimizing level differences. In common with developments elsewhere in the city, there are also guidelines to ensure that the underground links meet minimum width and height requirements to provide a spacious environment while catering for the expected footfall. Other aspects of safety and comfort are addressed by codes and guidelines on wayfinding and signage design, lighting levels, ventilation requirements and fire-safety measures.

Beyond Marina Bay, underground pedestrian networks and links have been planned in other areas, including built-up areas such as Orchard Road and the Civic District. For an existing development, this is often possible only with changes to existing floor plans. To minimize disruption, links are constructed incrementally — as part of the planning approval — when these sites undergo major works or redevelopment. In some cases, their construction is supported by a cash grant incentive scheme or initiatives such as GFA exemptions.

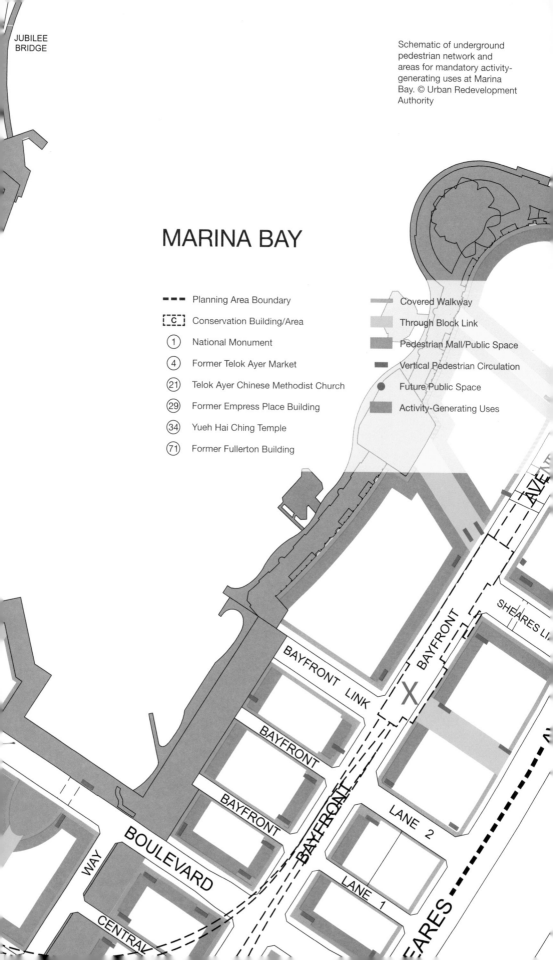

JUBILEE
BRIDGE

Schematic of underground
pedestrian network and
areas for mandatory activity-
generating uses at Marina
Bay. © Urban Redevelopment
Authority

MARINA BAY

- - - Planning Area Boundary
[C] Conservation Building/Area
(1) National Monument
(4) Former Telok Ayer Market
(21) Telok Ayer Chinese Methodist Church
(29) Former Empress Place Building
(34) Yueh Hai Ching Temple
(71) Former Fullerton Building

Covered Walkway
Through Block Link
Pedestrian Mall/Public Space
Vertical Pedestrian Circulation
● Future Public Space
Activity-Generating Uses

AVE

SHEARES LI

BAYFRONT LINK

BAYFRONT

BAYFRONT

BAYFRONT

LANE 2

BOULEVARD

LANE 1

WAY

CENTRAL

EARES

above: Immersive displays at the Singapore City Gallery
bring alive the planning challenges, and solutions to them.
© Urban Redevelopment Authority

Underground Master Plan

With such extensive underground development, there was a need
for a formalized plan to safeguard suitable underground spaces for
future uses. To this end, Singapore published its first underground
space plan focused on three pilot areas, namely Marina Bay, Punggol
Digital District and Jurong Innovation District, as part of the Draft
Master Plan of March 2019. Unlike the above-ground Master Plan,
which covers the allowable land use for every parcel island-wide,
this focuses on specific key areas with more extensive underground
uses. In addition to coordinating the shallow underground uses in
key districts, it will also safeguard corridors for future underground
infrastructure and areas for potential cavern development.

The underground space plan is three-dimensional — the first such
plan in the world — and provides information on both existing and
planned underground uses within the key areas. Identifying concealed
underground space — a capacity that is especially valuable in areas
with extensive underground uses — the 3D visualization makes it
easier to navigate within the actual usable underground space. It
allows for more precision in locating the space required, minimizing
unnecessary sterilization of land and space. It also serves as a control
plan, guiding landowners and developers in their planning and design
work by clearly showing the underground planning requirements and
constraints in the key areas. This will facilitate the development of the
underground spaces down the road, guided by needs, timing and the
economic and technical feasibility of the uses.

In addition to having a robust planning process, Singapore also has a structured research and development program that systematically identifies the challenges and coordinates nationwide efforts in going underground. One initiative, set up in 2017, is the Ministry of National Development's "Cities of Tomorrow" program, which, among other research objectives, aims to develop solutions that could improve the cost-effectiveness of constructing and operating underground facilities, creating new spaces and optimizing the space that Singapore currently has. The Singapore City Gallery, based at the URA Center, showcases the city-state's dramatic transformation over the past 50 years. Some 40 interactive and immersive exhibits bring the planning challenges — and innovative solutions — alive for the general public.

As Singapore continues to develop, the underground will play an important role as part of a larger system to provide the capacity for sustainable urban living. Singapore's approach to underground development has been shaped by learning best practices from other cities around the world and applying them as relevant to Singapore's circumstances.

" A Whole of Nation approach will be needed to optimize the use of land on the surface and the space beneath. Assuming that half of the territory is suitable for underground development we can double the space that we use ... We can further advance this frontier by daring to dream and do, by not being afraid to go into territories that others have not gone to. We must have belief in our young to do great things when they are trusted to dream, do and deliver. "

Professor Lui Pao Chuen
Advisor to Singapore's Ministry of National Development

TOKYO: OPENING MARUNOUCHI TO THE WORLD

Kentaro Furuya, Mitsubishi Jisho Sekkei Inc.

right: History of Marunouchi
Underground Space.
© Mitsubishi Jisho Sekkei Inc.

Marunouchi is one of the oldest and most prestigious business and commercial districts in Tokyo, internationally famous for the bustling underground city that runs parallel and connects to the one above ground. While Marunouchi's historical significance dates back over 400 years, its most radical transformation has taken place over the past century, led by its first private-sector real estate developer, Mitsubishi Estate Company. Adding underground space as an extra and vibrant dimension of the city has required visionary master planning and geotechnical feats, underpinned by an effective framework for aligning public and private sectors towards an urban vision that balances economic, cultural and environmental considerations.

The name Marunouchi literally means "within the circle," reflecting the district's origins inside the moats of Edo Castle, home to some of Japan's most powerful feudal lords. Today, the same 120ha of land — flanked on one side by the Imperial Palace and on the other by Tokyo Station, the country's largest transportation hub — hosts about 100 buildings occupied by some 4,000 enterprises employing 230,000 people. The whole district is integrated physically and conceptually, providing services and experiences that draw non-business visitors and further diversify its role as the economic and cultural core of Japan's capital city.

The Mitsubishi Estate Company, the largest landowner in Marunouchi, has led this holistic development, together with Mitsubishi Jisho Sekkei Inc., its architectural and engineering design subsidiary. Their transformation of Marunouchi has unfolded in three distinct phases, with a vision that has been built up layer upon layer over time.

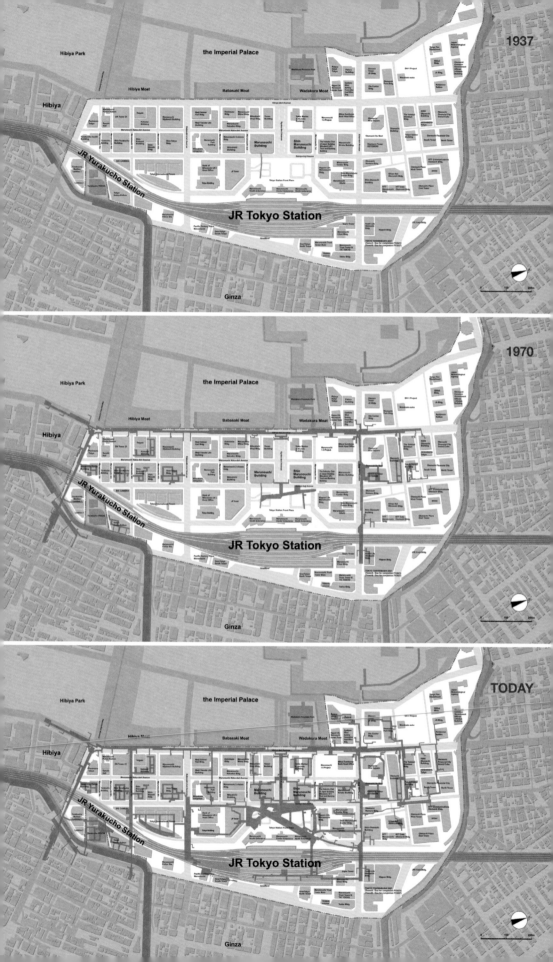

Transformation in Three Phases

Phase One: Launch of Japan's First Office Space

After the Meiji Restoration in 1868, the government reform of land laws to recognize private ownership heralded a new era in the nation's economic development. When land in Marunouchi was put up for sale in 1890, the Mitsubishi Company took the opportunity to purchase 3.5ha.[1] This would become the site of the first office building in Japan, Mitsubishi Ichigokan, also known as Mitsubishi No. 1 Building. Designed in a red brick European style, it set the tone for the new Tokyo Station, opened in 1914, and for other office buildings, giving rise to what became known as the "London Block" or the "red brick district." The presence of Tokyo Station made the surrounding area increasingly attractive for office space, initiating a period of high-rise construction unified at a height of 31m — the maximum permitted by the Urban Building Law of 1919. The signature feature of this fresh phase of development, the "New York Block," was the Marunouchi Building, which on its completion in 1923 was Japan's first mixed-use office and commercial building.

Tokyo Station, a strategically significant node connecting the district to more of the city and the city in turn to more of the nation, was also the starting point for the underground development of Marunouchi, with the construction in 1937 of the first underground corridor connecting the station with the Marounuchi Building.

above: View of Marunouchi around 1960.
Photo © Mitsubishi Estate

left: View of Marunouchi around 1890.
Photo © Mitsubishi Estate

Phase Two: Expansion for Economic Growth

The rapid growth of Japan's economy and the urgent demand for more office space in the Marunouchi area precipitated the second phase of the transformation. Between 1959, when the Marunouchi Remodeling Plan was formulated, and the early 1980s, an integrated approach ensured that the redevelopment of existing buildings ran in parallel with the widening of roads, inclusion of greenbelts and consolidation of city blocks. Although building regulations now permitted heights in excess of 100m, Marunouchi was careful to maintain a harmonious balance between its function as a business center and its location next to the impressive landscape of the historic Imperial Palace. During this second phase, the underground network for pedestrians started to take shape, with the construction of corridors connecting the new metro stations. But after several fire incidents in the 1970s, the development of underground space in Tokyo was virtually frozen till around 2000. As Marunouchi prepared to enter the new millennium, however, vertical development extending underground had begun to feature in Mitsubishi's thinking as much as above-ground and horizontal expansion.

above: View of Marunouchi around 2010.
Photo © Martin Holtkamp

Phase Three: Transformation into a Multi-functional, Interactive City

In 1995 the announcement of the redevelopment of the Marunouchi Building marked the beginning of the third phase that continues to this day and is defined by a people-oriented focus. If the earlier phases were concerned with providing new capacity through buildings and urban infrastructure, the guiding compass for this new phase is the idea of giving people enhanced urban experiences through designs that emphasize social interaction, green, energy-saving measures, and a plurality of functions as key themes. The initial six projects were mainly around Tokyo Station. Alongside the redevelopment of the flagship Marunouchi Building to accommodate new commercial facilities and office space, Marunouchi's unique approach to transit-oriented development allowed for the rapid expansion of the underground pedestrian network. By 2012 Mitsubishi Jisho Sekkei had designed approximately 90 percent of the underground space in Marunouchi developed after 2000. The aspiration is to make the district a global business hub, open to the world. Although buildings have become taller — the new Marunouchi Building is 180m — the focus on welcoming their users to interact with them has been maintained by locating shops, restaurants and cafes at street level.

In this phase, Mitsubishi has implemented a total design framework that engages all key stakeholders, with a systematic approach to connecting people with places via passageways and signage.

Total Design

The synergy of Marunouchi's cityscape is reflected in its integrated planning, which extends vertically and horizontally, above and below ground, according to an urban structure of zones, axes and hubs. Such integration is only possible when rules are established and observed by all stakeholders across public and private sectors. To make this possible, the Otemachi-Marunouchi-Yurakucho District Redevelopment Project Council was established in 1988 to bring together private developers and public authorities and facilitate cooperation on city planning. Research by the City Planning Institute of Japan on future visions of urbanism laid the groundwork for the Basic City Planning Agreement in 1994, followed by the formation of an advisory committee on area development in 1996. Two years later, in 1998, a series of development guidelines were enacted that are still in force today.

The Underground

At ground level, comfortable pedestrian-oriented environments run seamlessly throughout the Marunouchi district, while free shuttle buses provide road connections to subway stations. The congestion-free above-ground environment owes much to the successful underground development, which has reduced the need for private cars and established the underground layers of the district as appealing alternatives for businesses and consumers.

As Marunouchi grew above ground, its rail and metro systems expanded to handle the increased numbers of people traveling into and across the district. Today Marunouchi is connected by 13 stations — among them Tokyo, Yurakucho, Hibiya, Nijubashimae and Otemachi — and is the intersection for 20 railway lines. The growth of the sub-surface transportation network was in turn the catalyst for the construction of an underground city that maps Marunouchi's horizontal expansion above ground. In Mitsubishi's vision, subterranean space is designed to provide a variety of functions that support and entertain people, rather than simply serving as a means of circulation for a population in transit.

above: Tokyo Station Square
Photos © Martin Holtkamp

left: Sunken garden entrance to Shin Marunouchi Building.
Photo © Martin Holtkamp

The comfortable pedestrian routes on the surface are mirrored by an extensive system of underground passageways that form a pedestrian network connecting buildings to each other and to stations. From Otemachi at the northern end of the district through Marunouchi, and then from Yurakucho to Higashi-Ginza, where the Ginza Kabukiza Theater is located, continuously connected underground passageways provide an alternative indoor walking route. This allows people to travel safely, efficiently and comfortably around the district underground, taking in the facilities and experiences provided by the strategic combination and placement of transit-oriented developments.

Strategy and Structure of Underground Space

Marunouchi's underground pedestrian network may be huge, but it can be broken down into three major types of space: public squares, public underground passageways and private underground passages. Public squares are large open spaces directly adjoining stations and serving as central circulation nodes of the underground network. The second category of underground space is the network of public pedestrian corridors that run parallel to roads above

above: Sunken Garden of Mitsubishi UFJ Trust and
Banking/The Industry Club of Japan Building.
Photo © Koshi Miwa

ground and enable people to move through the district and between
stations, public squares and private buildings. The third category is
the underground passageways that link private buildings to public
underground passageways, enabling users to walk seamlessly
from the basement of their building to the platform of their train or
metro and to use the diversity of facilities in the sub-surface layers
of Marunouchi. The transition between underground and above-
ground space is achieved via intermediate spaces that are designed
to integrate connectivity and experience, offering shops, galleries,
greenery, street furniture such as benches and sculptures, sunken
gardens and outdoor cafes.

Underground Public Squares
Marunouchi's underground squares or plazas host a diversity of
events and occupants, such as pop up stores for new brands and
local specialty products, engaging and capitalizing on the busy flow
of people traveling between home and office. A prime example of this
is Marunouchi Station Square. Developed in three phases through a
public–private partnership between 2002 and 2012, its purpose was
to transform the underground walkway into a public plaza that would
be the gateway to Tokyo Station and a setting for public events and
services such as tourist information. To create this large underground
plaza, existing railway facilities and sewage pipes were re-routed.
Now the JR Tokyo Station, metro stations and basement floors of
adjacent buildings are seamlessly connected and an area that used to
be merely a station concourse has become a bustling place of activity
in itself.

Underground Public Corridors and Private Passageways

Connecting the Imperial Palace and Tokyo Station, Gyoko Avenue is both the urban and cultural spine of Marunouchi and one of the most famous public corridors in Tokyo as a whole, a route for the Imperial Cavalry on special occasions. Mitsubishi Jisho Sekkei decided to expand this prime urban axis by converting the public parking space under Gyoko Avenue into a parallel avenue underground, with a 220m-wide pedestrian concourse lined on either side by gallery space displaying art exhibitions for the enjoyment of visitors. At ground level, four rows of gingko trees were planted to echo the avenue's original design. The mechanical, engineering and public health (MEP) conduits and pipes for the parking were re-routed behind the new gallery space. Large planting pots, to hold the gingko trees above ground, were also installed in the MEP space. To blend the above-ground and underground environments, the lighting of the main concourse is designed with fixtures of several different color temperatures that are synchronized with the change of natural light from morning to evening outdoors. The ceiling of the staircase leading up to ground level is a glass skylight to enhance the feeling of openness to the sky while still providing shelter to those surfacing from the underground levels. The stone is the same as that used for the above-ground avenue and adjacent buildings, to preserve the historic context of this symbolically important avenue of Marunouchi.

Reflecting a different but equally critical set of considerations, Mitsubishi Jisho Sekkei's redevelopment of the underground passage running from Ginza Kabukiza Theater to Higashi-Ginza subway station involved the expansion of the station facilities, the installation of a new exit to street level and the extension of the underground passage in the Ginza direction. The renewal of this facility helps to alleviate rush-hour congestion and provides rain protection for theater-goers. The interior of the passage has been designed to match the adjoining underground plaza, Kobiki-cho Plaza, and to create a unified atmosphere with the Ginza Kabukiza Theater. The plaza also doubles as an emergency shelter, providing enhanced resiliency for the neighborhood.

In the same vein, redevelopment of the Palace Hotel Tokyo/Palace Building included an underground pedestrian route extending 100m to connect with Otemachi Station, one of the closest subway access points to the Imperial Palace. This underground passage has a distinctive atmosphere, defined by stone and wood panels that resonate with the interiors of the Palace Hotel.

Gyoko Underground Avenue. Photo © Martin Holtkamp

Signage System Design

Navigating around Marunouchi's underground urban complex is made easy by an integrated signage system. Mitsubishi mandates that the designs and information displayed on signs for public spaces are compliant with a specially developed "sign design book" that defines a unified rule for the font and picture sign system across the district. In all the underground carparks in Marunouchi, for example, the location and visibility of notices is consistent. In addition, the general rule of using monotone helps users to recognize that any signage in red or yellow requires special attention. The principle underpinning the whole system is that signs should be user-friendly to people of any nationality, gender and age, helping to fulfill the vision of "openness to the world."

A Society with Real Value

From Marunouchi's very first office building, Mitsubishi Ichigokan (Mitsubishi No. 1 Building) to the present day, more than 100 buildings later, Mitsubishi Jisho Sekkei has been intimately connected with this important district in the heart of Tokyo. Though much has changed since it developed its first building on its first plot of land more than a century ago, Mitsubishi's core value of contributing to "a society with real value" has remained steadfast and fueled its vision and decisions. It has enabled Mitsubishi to provide those who come

to Marunouchi with a holistic and positive experience of the district, seamlessly interwoven into the fabric of their lives: from home to work, across public and private spaces, from outdoor to indoor, and from above to below ground.

above: Night view of the Sunken Garden of Mitsubishi UFJ Trust and Banking/ The Industry Club of Japan Building. Photo © Koshi Miwa

REFLECTIONS FOR THE FUTURE

Mohsen Mostafavi, Harvard Graduate School of Design

Some of the most evocative images of the underground belong to the time of the Blitz in London in the early 1940s, when many of the city's subway stations were used as air raid shelters. Black and white photographs show thousands of people — the young, the elderly, many families with children — occupying the station platforms and tracks as makeshift places of safety from the bombing. The Underground operated during the day as normally as it could, and at night became a place of refuge. A new system of organization had to be invented to accommodate these temporary underground cities. Innovation is often a response to extreme conditions. Then, the transformation of the underground into places to "live in" was forced by the savage consequences of war. Today, rapid urbanization and climate change are opening up a new dimension of research and exploration linked to the future of the underground.

Still, those photos of the Blitz, with their contrast between the vivid humanity of the people and the harsh artificiality of the underground, remain as one the most potent representations of the challenge facing designers and engineers concerned with the creation of new kinds of subterranean environments. After all, we expect humans to live on land, in reach of light and air, and not within the confines of a man-made space hundreds of feet below ground.

Prior to its more recent history as infrastructure, the underground was most notably connected to the imaginary through mining, as the spaces of extraction and labor. An exemplary demonstration of what Lewis Mumford termed a "manufactured environment," the mine is a place that continues its "undistracted" operations day and night. With its relentless activities in aid of material production, it is invariably associated with pain and suffering, and not with pleasure and delight. However, subsequent technological and spatial developments of the underground to provide the infrastructure of modern life have changed our perception of the possibilities that lie ahead. Going beyond the two sides of the narrative historically associated with the

above: London's underground, then and now. Aldwych station during
the 1940 Blitz (left). Photo © Imperial War Museum (HU 44272).
New Crossrail line under construction (right). Photo AECOM

"underworld"— as both a place of refuge and a source of imminent
danger — the enabling and often invisible domain of the underground
is now inseparable from the daily activities of our cities, from
transportation, to electricity, to communications.

In the late 1950s and early 1960s the visionary Japanese Metabolist
architect Kiyonori Kikutake responded to the increasing shortage of
land in Tokyo with a series of proposals for vertical cities in the ocean.
More than half a century later, rather than constructing Kikutake's
vision of a Marine City, Tokyo is systematically moving below ground.
Kikutake's vision may still be realized, but in the meantime the idea of
the metropolis has become distinctly sectional, moving both below
and above ground. This ambivalent treatment of the ground has
enabled designers to create activities on multiple levels in ways never
imagined in the past. In part these spaces attempt to emulate the
environmental conditions above ground — of light and air, of water
and greenery. But another way to view the potential of these spaces
is to appreciate, even desire, their artificiality. What type of sensorial
regime could the underground construct that would complement,
rather than imitate, what lies above?

Increasingly, and with technology's assistance, the underground
is seen as a place of shelter from the untamable elements of
nature, such as extremes of heat or cold. But it is also a hermetic
place where any activity, from the theater to shopping, can unfold
unhindered, without distraction. The underground is a type of
"bracketed space" that can assume qualities different from the norms
that exist above ground. This place outside normalcy is also a space
of opportunity, open to unexpected and unimagined possibilities that
go beyond infrastructure and retail. The artificiality of the underground
provides the framework for the exploration of new experiential and
sensory conditions, both unique and in dialogue with the rest of the
metropolis. How to give expression to these new conditions? That is
the challenge for the future.

CONTRIBUTORS

EXECUTIVE SPONSOR AND FOREWORD

Sean Chiao is President, Asia Pacific, at AECOM. With over 30 years of experience in urban design and management, Sean has played a pivotal role in the creation of award-winning master plans for high-density new towns and the revitalization of existing urban landscapes, including the Kuala Lumpur River of Life; Delhi Mumbai Industrial Corridor; Bonifacio Global City in Metro Manila; and Suzhou Industrial Park. He is a Fellow of the American Institute of Architects (FAIA). In 2016, Sean spearheaded the publication of Jigsaw City, which showcases AECOM's work and philosophies around forming new urban environments and experiences in Asian cities. He has also orchestrated AECOM's collaboration with various institutions, including academia and the public sector, to explore topical issues related to Asia's rapid urbanization and to inspire the creation of tangible, holistic solutions.

EDITORS

Pamela Johnston is a London-based editor who works with architects and architectural schools and institutions around the world. For more than two decades she was Editor of AA Publications at the Architectural Association. Independently, she has collaborated with Princeton University Press, the Architecture Foundation in London, Aga Khan Trust for Culture in Geneva, Strelka Press in Moscow and the Milan-based San Rocco magazine, among many others. Recent titles include Peter Märkli: Everything one invents is true (Quart Verlag) and OFFICE Kersten Geers David Van Severen vols. 1 & 3 (Koenig Books). Forthcoming titles include a survey of the work of Florian Beigel and the Architecture Research Unit, for which she was awarded a Graham Foundation grant.

Nancy F. Lin is the head of Strategy & Growth and Chief of Staff for AECOM's Asia Pacific President. She is a civil engineer, architect and urban designer with over 20 years of experience in urban design, architecture, landscape design, construction administration and project management for architectural projects involving collaboration among multi-disciplinary and international teams. Before joining AECOM, Nancy taught for 12 years at various universities, served as an advisor to city governments, and has lectured and published widely in Taiwan. She continuously promotes collaboration with academia across Greater China and Southeast Asia. Nancy is a Registered Architect of New York; a Member of the American Institute of Architects; a Member of the Board for the Chinese Institute of Urban Design in Taiwan; and a Founding Member of the Organization of Architecture Reformation in Taiwan.

TECHNICAL EDITOR

John Endicott is an AECOM Fellow in recognition of more than 40 years of excellence in ground engineering. He heads AECOM's geotechnical practice in the Asia Pacific region. John studied at Cambridge University, completing a PhD in 1970 on the deformation of slopes, and is now a Fellow Commoner at St. Catharine's College. In 1975 he went to Hong Kong to work on tender designs for MTR underground railway contracts that were pioneering soil/ structure interaction. He has been based in Hong Kong ever since. He has continued to work on underground railway projects and contributed to the design of more than 100 underground station structures.

A NEW FRONTIER

Mark Pimlott is an artist, designer, writer and teacher. He is the author of The Public Interior as Idea and Project (Rotterdam: Episode Publishers, 2016), In passing (Heijningen: Jap Sam Books, 2010) and Without and Within: Essays on Territory and the Interior (Heijningen: Jap Sam Books, 2007). His practice, concerned with appearances, experience, meaning, and reconciliations with time, incorporates photography, art for public places and architectural design. Notable works are "World" at BBC Broadcasting House, London (2013); "La Scala," Aberystwyth (2003); and interiors of the Red House, London (2001; 2011, with Tony Fretton architects). His work has been exhibited internationally, including at the Venice Architecture Biennale (2010). He lives and works in The Hague, and is currently Assistant Professor in the Chair of Interiors Buildings Cities, Department of Architecture, Faculty of Architecture and the Built Environment at Delft University of Technology, the Netherlands.

Ilkka Vähäaho has more than 40 years' experience in foundation and rock engineering at the City of Helsinki, where he has been Head of the Geotechnics Division since 1997. As a "Global Perspective Ambassador" of ITACUS (International Tunneling and Underground Space Association's Committee on Underground Space), he is engaged in promoting the usefulness of underground resources. His most recent publications on the underground spaces of Helsinki can be downloaded via the following links: www.bit.ly/urban-underground-space and www.bit.ly/underground-spaces. He has been closely involved in the development of numerous national and European standards and in the work of the Finnish Geotechnical Society SGY and the Finnish Tunneling Association MTR-FTA.

PEOPLE-CENTERED SPACES

Will Symons leads AECOM's Asia Pacific Sustainability & Resilience Practice and supports clients to make better decisions in the context of increasing complexity and uncertainty resulting from urbanization, globalization and climate change. His recent experience includes supporting nine cities across the region to develop their first resilience strategies as part of the 100 Resilient Cities initiative, including Jakarta, Bangkok, Singapore, Kyoto, Christchurch and Melbourne. He is leading the development and implementation of a BHP Foundation-funded coral reef resilience initiative for the Great Barrier Reef Foundation, focused on five world heritage marine sites in Australia, New Caledonia, Palau and Belize, and is leading the delivery of New Zealand's first National Climate Change Risk Assessment.

Lee Barker-Field joined AECOM in 2004, when he co-founded the lighting division, and he has been with the company ever since. With a Masters degree from the Bartlett Faculty of the Built Environment (University College London) and over 15 years' experience, he is a specialist in architectural lighting design and enhancement of the built environment through daylighting optimization. Now, as head of Lighting at AECOM, Lee has been the lead lighting designer for major projects on five continents and across all sectors. His projects range from large high-profile international commissions such as the lighting masterplan for the Rio 2016 Olympic Park, to temporary architecture including the annual Serpentine Pavilion installations (2013 to 2016).

MOVING PEOPLE, TRANSPORTING GOODS

Carlos López Galviz is co-editor, with Bradley L. Garrett and Paul Dobraszcyk, of Global Undergrounds: Exploring Cities Within (2016) and the author of Cities, Railways, Modernities: London, Paris, and the Nineteenth Century (2019). A lecturer in the Theory and Methods of Social Futures at Lancaster University, his work looks at futures thinking and future forming through the lens of cities, ruins and infrastructure. He has studied cities like London, Paris and Shanghai, using history as a means of thinking about what theories and which methods are relevant to understanding their future today and in the past.

NEW TECHNIQUES OF REPRESENTATION

Ville 10D – Ville d'Idées (10D City – City of Ideas) is a French National Research Project that was set up in 2012 to explore ways of extending the use of the underground to contribute to a more sustainable form of urban development. Bringing together around 30 researchers from a range of disciplines, it has created analytical tools for approaching key issues of underground urbanism. **Monique Labbé** is an architect and founder of Les Ateliers Monique Labbé. She is General Director of the Ville 10D National Research Project and former President (2005–17) of the Underground Space Committee, AFTES (French Tunneling and Underground Space Association). **Jean-Pierre Palisse** is an architect and urban planner and Executive Director of Ville 10D and former Deputy President (1998–2013) of IAU-IdF (Institut d'aménagement et d'urbanisme de la Région Ile-de-France). **Jean-François David** is an architect and BIM expert at Les Ateliers Monique Labbé.

Thomson Lai is AECOM's Greater China Digital Transformation Team Leader, overseeing the Digital Solutions and Digital Transformation practice to drive the adoption of digital technology across the region. With over 20 years of experience, he is a veteran in the geospatial industry and is a chartered surveyor, member of the Hong Kong Institute of Building Information Modeling (HKIBIM), and a Project Management Professional (PMP) certified project manager. As a trained practitioner, Thomson has pioneered the integration of new technologies — including BIM, GIS, photogrammetry, IoT and immersive technology — in a number of transformational civil infrastructure projects.

Roger Luo is Associate, Virtual Design and Construction (VDC), Innovative Solutions at AECOM. As a Hong Kong-based electronic and information engineer with a comprehensive knowledge of management, planning and coordination in the Architecture, Engineering and Construction industry, he is responsible for the successful completion of Building Information Modeling (BIM) projects. Roger has 15 years' experience in BIM and nearly 20 years' experience using the latest in advanced technology to deliver innovative and inspiring solutions to AECOM and its clients in Hong Kong and throughout the Asia Pacific region.

Jeffrey Chun-fai Wong is a Senior Geotechnical Engineer in the Geotechnical Engineering Office (GEO), Civil Engineering and Development Department of the Hong Kong Special Administrative Region Government. He joined the GEO after graduating from the University of Hong Kong with a bachelor degree in Earth Sciences in 1996. A Chartered Geologist, he has undertaken a range of projects on geological studies, landslide mapping, slope design and cavern development, and is currently a core member of the multidisciplinary Pilot Study on Underground Space Development in Selected Strategic Urban Areas with AECOM Asia Company Limited as the Consultants.

Tan Tin-lun Yeung is a Geotechnical Engineer in the Geotechnical Engineering Office (GEO), Civil Engineering and Development Department of the Hong Kong Special Administrative Region Government. He graduated from the Hong Kong University of Science and Technology in 2007 with BEng in Civil and Structural Engineering and obtained MSc degree in Engineering from the University of Hong Kong in 2010. He has been involved in a range of projects including slope upgrading and natural terrain hazard mitigation, site formation and ELS works, and was a core member of the multidisciplinary Pilot Study on Underground Space Development in Selected Strategic Urban Areas with AECOM Asia Company Limited.

LOOKING FORWARD

Peter Ho is Chairman of the Urban Redevelopment Authority of Singapore. He is also Senior Advisor to the Centre for Strategic Futures and a Senior Fellow in the Civil Service College. When he retired from the Singapore Administrative Service in 2010 after a career stretching more than 34 years, he was Head, Civil Service, concurrent with his other appointments of Permanent Secretary (Foreign Affairs), Permanent Secretary (National Security and Intelligence Coordination) and Permanent Secretary (Special Duties) in the Prime Minister's Office. Before that, he was Permanent Secretary (Defense). He is the author of The Challenges of Governance in a Complex World, which collects the four Institute of Policy Studies – S. R. Nathan public lectures he delivered in 2017.

The Urban Redevelopment Authority (URA) is Singapore's land use planning and conservation agency. Our mission is "to make Singapore a great city to live, work and play." We strive to create an endearing home and a vibrant city through long-term planning and innovation, in partnership with the community. URA's multi-faceted role includes being the main government land sales agent. We attract and channel private capital investments to develop sites that support planning, economic and social objectives. We also partner the community to enliven our public spaces to create a car-lite, people-friendly and livable city for all to enjoy. In shaping a distinctive city, URA also promotes architecture and urban design excellence. Visit www.ura. gov.sg for more information.

Teo Tiong Yong is currently the Group Director (Project Management) of JTC Corporation, the lead agency responsible for the development of industrial infrastructure to support and catalyze the growth of new industries and transform existing enterprises in Singapore. In his current role Tiong Yong oversees the project management for all JTC, Ministry of Trade & Industry and selected government agencies building and infrastructure projects. He was involved in the Ministry of Defense's Underground Ammunition Facility cavern and Public Utilities Board's Deep Tunnel Sewerage System, and was also the lead Project Manager for JTC's Jurong Rock Caverns (JRC). He continues to play the key role of an underground caverns domain specialist in JTC. Tiong Yong is a Singapore Registered Professional Engineer and a registered Chartered Engineer (Infrastructure Engineering and Project Management) under the Institution of Engineers, Singapore.

Kentaro Furuya is Deputy General Manager of the International Business Planning department at Mitsubishi Jisho Sekkei Inc. After obtaining a Master of Architecture degree from Washington University in St. Louis he worked for HOK in San Francisco and Seattle, subsequently joining Mitsubishi Jisho Sekkei Inc. in 2004. As an architect, he has worked on healthcare, senior living and office projects in the United States and Japan. Between 2015 and 2018 he was stationed in Singapore to help with the establishment of Mitsubishi Jisho Sekkei Asia, enabling him to participate in various types of work throughout Southeast Asia, from small refurbishments to large-scale master planning.

REFLECTIONS FOR THE FUTURE

Mohsen Mostafavi, architect and educator, is the Alexander and Victoria Wiley Professor of Design and Harvard University Distinguished Service Professor. He served as Dean of the GSD from 2008 to 2019. He was formerly the Gale and Ira Drukier Dean of the College of Architecture, Art and Planning at Cornell University and, before that, Chairman of the Architectural Association School of Architecture in London. His work focuses on modes and processes of urbanization and on the interface between technology and aesthetics. He is a consultant on a number of international architectural and urban projects, and his research and design projects have been published in many journals. His books include Ecological Urbanism (co-edited 2010 and recently translated into Chinese, Portuguese and Spanish); In the Life of Cities (2012); Portman's America & Other Speculations (2017) and Ethics of the Urban: The City and the Spaces of the Political (2017).

ILLUSTRATOR

Jason Ho is a graduate of University College London, where he attained a Master of Architecture with distinction, and was also awarded the Bartlett Medal and the Fitzroy Robinson Drawing Prize. His works have received high commendation from renowned architectural and art organizations and have featured on the cover of the RIBA Journal. His drawings were exhibited in the Royal Academy of Art's 2019 Summer Exhibition, and his collaborative work with Professor C.J. Lim was exhibited at Roca London Gallery. As an illustrator, Jason explores spaces where art, architecture and imagination collide, through the making of complete, immersive alternative realities. His illustrations unfold stories about technology, nature, sustainability and communities, with entrancing details hidden within the layered narrative.

REFERENCES

A NEW FRONTIER

Experimental Cities

1   Quotations in this section are taken principally from Athelstan Spilhaus, "The Experimental City," Daedalus 96:4 (Fall 1967), 1129–41. Other sources are Athelstan Spilhaus, "Why have Cities?," The Science Teacher 3:9 (December 1969) and "The Experimental City," a documentary by Chad Freidrichs (2017).

2   Quoted in www.avivremagazine.fr/guy-rottier-architecte-libre-a39

3   Ibid.

4   A building that coincidentally has been associated with Fourier's phalanstery in its form and its desire to mold human behavior through architecture.

5   Quoted in Nadine Labedade, www.frac-centre.fr/collection-art-architecture/rub/rubauteurs-58. html?authID=164

6   See preface to Manfredo Tafuri, Architecture and Utopia (Cambridge, MA: MIT Press, 1973).

Montreal: The Ville Intérieure as Prototype for the Continuous Interior

1   Eric Mumford, Sarkis, Josep Lluís Sert: The Architect of Urban Design 1953–1969 (New Haven: Yale University Press, 2008). Zeckendorf and Pei had a track record with regard to questions of the "heart of the city," developing several urban renewal projects in the United States, notably the Mile High Center in Denver, Colorado (1956) and Washington Square East in Philadelphia (1960) that worked with the scale of the historical fabric while reordering automobile traffic and the public realm.

2   Vincent Ponte, "Man, Buildings, New Dimensions for Downtown," Skyscraper Management, 52:12 (1967), 11–36.

3   Victor Gruen, The Heart of Our Cities: The Urban Crisis, Diagnosis and Cure
(New York: Simon & Schuster, 1964).

4   Peter Wolf, "The First Modern Urbanist: Eugène Hénard," Architectural Forum,
October 1967, 50–55.

5   As publicized in the New York Herald Tribune; Alison Sky, Michelle Stone, Unbuilt America: Forgotten Architecture in America from Thomas Jefferson to the Space Age
(New York: McGraw-Hill, 1976).

6   Interview with the author at the offices of Pei Cobb Freed, February 2011.

7   Webb & Knapp (Canada) Ltd., Ville-Marie Master Plan (1955).

8   André Lortie, "Montreal 1960: The Singularity of a Metropolitan Archetype," André Lortie (ed.), The 60s: Montréal Thinks Big (Montreal: CCA, 2004), 75–115. The plan notably incorporates key structural elements of Jacques Gréber's plan of 1953, in the spirit of the City Beautiful movement.

9   William Zeckendorf, Zeckendorf: The Autobiography of a Man who Played a Real-Life Game of Monopoly and Won the Biggest Real Estate Game in History
(New York: Holt Reinhart Winston, 1970).

10 The motorway and its spur, terminating in Place Bonaventure, were completed in 1967.

11 Interview between the author and Henry N. Cobb, New York, February 2011.

12 After an extensive renovation in the late 1980s, these spaces were filled with food courts and roofed over. The promenade's architectural features completely changed to resemble a conventional mall, while the uniform signage system was replaced to conform with the demands of the "free market." The place above was converted to a park with raised beds, lawns and trees, as designed by the project's original executive architects, ARCOP.

13 Victor Gruen's 1956 Southdale Center in Medina, Minnesota, was the first indoor shopping mall and established what would become the most-influential building type of the latter half of the twentieth century. It is still potent today in its deployment in shopping developments, airports, museums, etc.

14 In this respect, its imagery reflected tendencies arising in the American laissez-faire conditions of the late 1950s that connected shopping centers to workplaces. For a more extensive discussion of this, see Mark Pimlott, Without and Within: Essays on Territory and the Interior (Rotterdam: Episode Publishers, 2007).

15 The programming was planned by the architects within the development company framework, and notably by a key publicist in the team, Nelly McLean. Pei Cobb Freed archives, New York.

16 Derek Drummond, "In Praise of Modernist Civic Spaces in Canadian Cities," Policy Options, February 2004, 53–58.

17 Raymond T. Affleck, "Celebration of the Mixmaster," Modulus 5 (1968), University of Virginia, 62–70.

18 Reyner Banham, Megastructures: Urban Futures of the Recent Past (New York: Harper & Row, 1976).

19 Eva Vescei, project architect of Place Bonaventure; interview with the author, 11 July 2011, at the rooftop garden of Place Bonaventure, Montreal.

20 Peter Blake, "Downtown in 3D," Architectural Forum, 125:2 (September 1966), 69–75.

21 The metro's construction coincided with that of Expo 67 and the excavations from the former were used as landfill for the expo site of two islands — one artificial and one extended — in the middle of the St. Lawrence River.

22 Norman Slater, Metro: Material and Finish Recommendation for Stations (Montreal: STM, 1964).

23 Victor Prus, "Place Bonaventure Metro Station, Montreal," Canadian Architect, August 1967, 45–48.

24 Isabelle Gournay, "Gigantism in Downtown Montreal," Montreal Metropolis 1880–1930 (Montreal: CCA, 1998), 152–82.

25 Exhibits and interior architecture were designed by Cambridge Seven Associates.

26 Of these, Habitat still reminds the city of its popular future as a fragment of Brutalist nostalgia, while the US pavilion is a shell accommodating a museum, the bubble consumed by flames in 1976, and Otto's translucent tent for West Germany — a prototype for the shelter of the 1972 Munich Olympic Stadium — collapsed under the weight of the first big snow after the closure of the exposition.

27 Reyner Banham, op. cit.; it was also the stated intention of the exhibition's organizers and the commissioner general, Pierre Dupuy, that Man and his World should serve as instruction and inspiration for the young, the future stewards of the planet. Expo 67 Guide officiel (1967).

28 Aspects of the Ponte plan were never realized. These included another east–west metro line north of Place Ville-Marie, which would have been the incentive for developments along the entire north–south axis of McGill College Avenue, connecting Place Ville-Marie visually and structurally to the city's most prominent geographical feature, Mont-Royal. Of further significance is Frederick Law Olmsted's design of Parc Mont-Royal (1877), which tied Montreal to the precepts of the City Beautiful movement, and which the MACE plan (1966), designed by I.M. Pei with Cobb and Ponte, would have honored.

Helsinki: City of Deep Collaborations

1 Helsinki City, "The Helsinki Underground Master Plan, Brochure, Urban Environment Division's Technical and Economic Planning Unit," 2009. Available at www.hel2.fi/ksv/julkaisut/esitteet/esite_2009-8_en.pdf

2 Formerly known as the Geotechnical Division of the Real Estate Department.

3 R. Sterling, H. Admiraal, N. Bobylev, H. Parker, J.P. Godard, I. Vähäaho, C.D.F. Rogers, X. Shi, T. Hanamura, "Sustainability Issues for Underground Space in Urban Areas," Proceedings of the ICE — Urban Design and Planning 165:4 (December 2012). DOI: 10.1680/udap.10.00020

4 Finnish Tunneling Association MTR-FTA, The Fourth Wave of Rock Construction, Environmentally Responsible Underground Design, Engineering and Application (Porvoo, WSOY 1997).

5 A. Saraste, "Kallioperäkartta' (Bedrock Map) GEO 10K, 1:10,000, City of Helsinki, Real Estate Department, Geotechnical Division, 1978.

6 The Suomalainen brothers moved to Hamina after the island that was their childhood home was ceded to the Soviet Union. See www.temppeliaukio.fi/english/

7 I. Satola, M. Riipinen, "Technical Services and Utility Tunnels in Helsinki," Proceedings of the World Tunnel Congress WTC–2011, Helsinki, Finland (extended abstract).

8 For further information see the Helsinki Regional Environmental Services Authority at www.hsy.fi/sites/Esitteet/EsitteetKatalogi/viikinmaki_tekninenesite_en.pdf

9 Detail for this section from Johanna Lemola; see www.globenewswire.com/news-release/2018/12/19/1669664/0/en/Helsinki-Produces-Energy-with-Underground-Hot-and-Cold-Water-Lakes.html

10 The Callio project is a collaboration between the town of Pyhäjärvi and the University of Oulu. https://process-sme.eu/2018/11/08/reuse-of-a-mine-callio-a-globally-unique-multidisciplinary-business-environment/

11 There is also another proposal to build the tunnel using private funding. FinEst Bay Area Development Ltd plans to open a rail traffic tunnel between Helsinki and Tallinn by 24 December 2024. See www.ymparisto.fi/download/noname/%7BC835F381-FC0B-42DA-8379-26A2E9693EAD%7D/145338

12 John F. Helliwell, Richard Layard and Jeffrey D. Sachs (eds.), World Happiness Report 2019. Four Nordic countries featured in the top five happiest nations, with Finland heading the table for the second year running.

PEOPLE-CENTERED SPACES

The Resilient City

1   https://www.publicspace.org/works/-/project/h034-water-square-in-benthemplein

Homo Subterraneus: Inhabiting the Subsurface

1   Mohammad Mahdi Safaee, "Shavadan: The Sustainable Architecture in the City of Dezful in Iran," Proceedings of the 12th World Conference of the Associated Research Centers for Urban Underground Space (ACUUS 2009).

2   The principal texts referred to here are: Adam C. Roberts, George I. Christopoulos, Josip Car, Chee Kiong-Soh, Ming Lu, "Psycho-biological factors associated with underground spaces: What can the new era of cognitive science offer to their study?," Tunnelling and Underground Space Technology 55 (2016), 118–34; Chee Kiong-Soh, George I. Christopoulos, Adam C Roberts, Eun-Hee Lee, "Human-centered development of underground work spaces," Procedia Engineering 165 (2016), 242–50; Chee-Kiong Soh, Vicknaeshwari Marimuther, Adam C. Roberts, Josip Car, Kian Woon Kwok, George I. Christopoulos, "Developing and Communicating High-Value, Human-Centered Underground Work Spaces: Results of a Multidisciplinary, Multi-Year Study," Proceedings of the 16th World Conference of the Associated Research Centers for the Urban Underground Space (ACUUS 2018), 10–19.

3   Steven W. Lockley, George C. Brainard, Charles A. Czeisler, "High sensitivity of the human circadian melatonin to resetting by short wavelength light," Journal of Clinical Endocrinology and Metabolism 88:9 (2003), 4502–05.

4   R. Küller and L. Wetterberg, "The subterranean work environment: impact on well-being and health," Environment International 22:1 (1996); quoted in Roberts et al., 2016.

5   M. Boubreki, I.N. Cheung et al., "Impact of windows and daylight exposure on overall health and sleep quality of office workers: a case-control pilot study," Journal of Clinical Sleep Medicine 10:6 (2014), includes a review of recent literature on this subject.

6   Susan Kessler, Quartz, 19 June 2017.
     https://qz.com/986215/your-new-office-lightbulbs-may-be-hacking-your-circadian-rhythms/

7   These notes on intensity of light and work performance are drawn directly from Roberts et al., Tunnelling and Underground Space Technology 55 (2016), 118–34.

8   I. Knez and N. Hygge, "Irrelevant speech and indoor lighting: effects on cognitive performance and self-reported affect," Applied Cognitive Psychology 16:6 (2002), quoted in Roberts et al.

9   Jeonghwan Kim, Seung Hyun Cha, Choongwan Koo, Shiu-keung Tang, "The effects of indoor plants and artificial windows in an underground environment," Building and Environment 138 (2018), 53–62.

10   Zheng Tan, Adam Charles Roberts, Eun Hee Lee, Georgios Christopoulos, Kian-Woon Kwok, Josip Car, Chee Kiong Soh, "Architectural Design, Perception and Health in Underground Working Environments," Proceedings of the 16th World Conference of the Associated Research Centers for the Urban Underground Space (ACUUS 2018), Hong Kong, 538–43.

11   LM Gil-Martín, A Peña-Garcia, A Jiménez, Enrique Hernández-Montes, "Study of light-pipes for the use of sunlight in road tunnels," Tunnelling and Underground Space Technology 41:1 (2014), 82–87.

12 The methodology is described in detail in Roberts et al., 2016.

13 Roberts et al., 2016.

14 Tim Edensor, From Light to Dark: Daylight, Illumination and Gloom (Minneapolis: University of Minnesota Press, 2017) examines the effects of daylight and darkness on our perception of our surroundings.

15 Interview with James Turrell, Financial Times, 24 May 2013.

Bringing the Elements of Nature Underground

ARoS Aarhus: Next Level Extension

1   Quotes from James Turrell are taken from a 2016 conversation between James Turrell, the architect David Adjaye and LACMA director Michael Govan available at https://archinect.com/news/article/149973813/watch-david-adjaye-and-james-turrell-discuss-light-space-and-architecture [accessed 21 October 2019]

MOVING PEOPLE, TRANSPORTING GOODS

Of Loops, Pumps, Pipes and Hype

1   See G.D. Hiscox, Compressed Air: Its Production, Uses and Applications … as Motive Power (London: Sampson Low, Marston, 1902).

2   The post was one of several underground pneumatic networks which included time "pulses," drainage and motive power; see, for example, Th. Poujol, Des réseaux pneumatiques dans la ville: un siècle et demi de techniques marginales (Noisy-le-Grand: Université de Paris-Val le Marne, 1986). François Truffaut's "Baisers volés" (1968) has a famous sequence showing the trajectory of a letter sent via the pneu.

3   This is taken from the report "The Pneumatic Service of the British Post Office Telegraphs," included in the Pneumatic Tubes radiating from the GPO West, 1910, available in the archives of the Postal Museum in London.

4   Included in the Historical Précis of the Report by the Committee on Pneumatic Tubes or Underground Electric Railways (1911), also available in the archives of the Postal Museum, London.

5   Reported by Hyperloop One in September 2017, see https://hyperloop-one.com/our-story#global-challenge-finalists [accessed 25 September 2018].

6   See the Warburg Institute's Iconographic Database, Gods and Myths, for a unique sample of representations of Atlas during the Renaissance and other periods: https://iconographic.warburg.sas.ac.uk/vpc/VPC_search/subcats.php?cat_1=5&cat_2=168 [accessed 12 October 2018]. Tintoretto's drawing is itself a study of a statuette of Atlas.

NEW TECHNIQUES OF REPRESENTATION

Reclaiming the Subterranean No Man's Land of Paris La Défense

1   All the more so since safety regulations have been tightened. Throughways, for instance, now fall under the regulatory category of tunnels.

LOOKING FORWARD

Hong Kong: A Matter of When, Not If or How

1   Quoted in T. Mellor, "The Cross-Harbour Tunnel – Part 1 Gestation," The Industrial History of Hong Kong Group, https://industrialhistoryhk.org/the-cross-harbour-tunnel-part-1-gestation/ [accessed 21 October 2019].

2   Cut and cover method of construction is when a long trench is excavated (cut) and tunnels are built from reinforced concrete within the deep trench. After, soil is placed over the tunnel, filling the trench back up to ground level (cover).

3   At Tai Koo, Sai Wan Ho, Sai Ying Pun, University, Lei Tung, Ho Man Tin and Admiralty Extension (South Island Line).

Singapore's Next Frontier: Going Underground

1   The Singapore Height Datum is pegged to the historical mean sea level and is the reference point for height measurements across the whole of Singapore.

2   NEWater is reclaimed water purified using dual-membrane and ultraviolet technologies, in addition to conventional water treatment processes.

First published in 2020 by Lund Humphries

Lund Humphries
Office 3, Book House
261A City Road
London EC1V 1JX
UK

www.lundhumphries.com

ISBN (paperback): 978-1-84822-358-5

A Cataloguing-in-Publication record for this book is available from the British Library.

Designed by Steve Kwok

Set in Helvetica Neue

Printed in Singapore